Secrets of the Setters

Hugh Stephenson is the *Guardian*'s crossword editor.

Secrets of the Setters

How to Solve the *Guardian* Crossword

Hugh Stephenson

theguardian

ATLANTIC BOOKS
LONDON

First published in Great Britain in hardback in 2005 by Atlantic Books on behalf of Guardian Newspapers Ltd. Atlantic Books is an imprint of Grove Atlantic Ltd.

This paperback edition published in 2007 by Atlantic Books on behalf of Guardian Newspapers Ltd.

ISBN 978 1 84354 469 2

A CIP record for this book is available from the British Library

10 9 8 7 6 5 4 3 2 1

Printed in Great Britain

Atlantic Books
An imprint of Grove Atlantic Ltd
Ormond House
26–27 Boswell Street
London WC1N 3JZ

To all the *Guardian*'s crossword setters, without whose wit and wisdom it would have been impossible to write this book.

Contents

Introduction

In the last interview he ever gave (to the University of Liverpool alumni magazine *Insight*), the broadcaster and journalist John Peel said this:

> My daughter, Flossy, always found me slightly embarrassing . . . She had always been quite reserved with me. In fact, it was the *Guardian* crossword and texting that really brought us closer together. I would be walking round London, my mobile would go and it would be Flossy. There was never any preamble, she'd just say: 'Writing desk, 10 letters' and I would say: 'That would be escritoire.' She would say thanks and then there would be a click. It's a small thing, but it brought us closer together.

'Escritoire', in this case, was a solution in a *Guardian* Quick crossword, but all crossword puzzles play unexpected social roles of this kind. They act as bonding agents in the staffroom or the pub. They help actors to kill time, when hanging around during rehearsals or waiting to go on. They are a ridiculously easy way of making strangers on a train think that you must be bright.

For this last purpose, you do not even have to be able to work out the clues. I have it on good authority – from an actor; it must, therefore, be true – that Sir John Gielgud was once rattling impressively through a cryptic crossword. Looking over his shoulder, someone asked: 'John, what is that word DIBNUTS that you've just filled in with such a flourish?' Thus was Sir John's failure to work out an anagram for DUSTBIN cruelly exposed.

A crossword is an unusual puzzle in that you can derive enjoyment from it, even if you cannot complete it entirely. Other puzzles, like the number-based Sudoku, say, leave you unsatisfied if you cannot get them to 'come out', but a crossword can give you ten minutes, half an hour, or an afternoon of satisfaction at having solved at least some of the clues, provided that the setter of the puzzle has shown wit, wisdom and elegance.

Of course, crosswords also suit those who thrive on competition. The *Guardian*, in common with almost all publications carrying crosswords, has prize puzzles, though the modesty of the prizes on offer shows that competing rather than winning is what counts. There are also competitions against the clock under examination conditions, where the winners solve the set puzzle in not much more time than it would take most of us to fill in the grid, if we knew the answers in advance.

With a crossword, though, the travelling hopefully gives most people quite as much pleasure as arriving at the terminus. Solving 25 per cent of a difficult puzzle can give just as much satisfaction as solving 100 per cent of an easy one. Here, an unusual feature of the *Guardian*'s cryptic crosswords is that they deliberately offer very different degrees of challenge to the solver. With the crosswords in most other publications, the setters are anonymous and the puzzles are pitched at a standard level. This is fine, if that particular level suits you, but it can be frustrating for beginners and boring for experts, unless they simply enjoy pitting themselves against the clock.

Since 1970, the cryptic crossword puzzles in the *Guardian* have carried the *noms de guerre* of their setters. You can see who you are up against, get to know each individual's little ways and have your favourites. It is, inevitably, a subjective judgement as to which setters are harder than others, but a rough grouping would probably put Bunthorne, Enigmatist, Paul, Shed and Taupi at the harder end of our daily scale and

Audreus, Janus, Logodaedalus, Quantum and Rufus at the other end, with the rest spread between. Araucaria is in something of a class of his own, since to a beginner he is hard. But, once solvers get accustomed to the length and direction of his bowling, they come to recognise that his clues are fair, outstandingly original and often funny.

This book is not written for the person who already does the cryptic crosswords in the *Guardian.* It is written for someone who is aware that others get pleasure from them and would like, in principle, to join in, but fears that the whole thing is too daunting and arcane. Its aim is to convince those hesitating on the brink that no abnormal intelligence is required to tackle and enjoy the puzzles that you will find daily in the paper, or on the *Guardian*'s website.

Certainly, there are conventions involved and the grammar of the cryptic crossword clue is not that of standard writing. Cryptic clues often depend on references to history and culture, both high and low. Proverbs and sayings, old and new songs, nursery rhymes, cricket and bridge terms, the Bible, Shakespeare, Lewis Carroll, Jane Austen, Charles Dickens and the Brontë sisters, actors dead and alive flit regularly through the clues. But, in general, the level of knowledge and familiarity required to come up with the right answer is the sort you might need in a pub quiz, rather than in Mastermind.

In the past, there has undoubtedly been a bias in our

puzzles in favour of the humanities and against science, in favour of the high and against the low brow. But, with the new generation of setters, that balance has been steadily shifting. Sometimes both the solutions and the clues are a touch esoteric. But, if the clues are fair, the process of getting to the right answer and of confirming it, if necessary, in some dictionary or other standard reference work (or via Google) can itself lead to interesting discoveries in previously unknown areas.

Perhaps because they are usually written by a crossword setter, most books with titles such as *How to Solve a Cryptic Crossword* seem to end up as books on how to set one, making much of the author's personal reflections as to what does and does not constitute a fair cryptic clue. This seems to be the wrong approach for beginners seeking guidance on how to tackle *Guardian* crosswords.

So this book is written firmly for those who would like to take the cryptic plunge, but do not know how or where to begin. My advice is that, having read this book, you should start with one or two of the less hard of the *Guardian* compilers and make a practice of looking up the answers to the clues you fail to solve in order to find out how they are supposed to work. I have throughout used actual clues by *Guardian* setters, crediting them by name (in square brackets).

You will find, surprisingly, that just a few minutes of

practice will produce results and that, the longer you keep at it, the better you will become. Remember also, as an added incentive, that there is clear medical evidence that solving crosswords helps to keep Alzheimer's at bay. So, too, I am told, does smoking, but crosswords have fewer side effects.

The first chapter is an account of the history of the cryptic puzzle. It can easily be skipped by those who want to get down to the real business.

One

A little bit of history

The invention of the modern crossword is generally credited to a man called Arthur Wynne, who was born in Liverpool in 1862 and whose first puzzle saw the light of day on Sunday, 21 December 1913 in the *New York World.*

This newspaper was founded in 1860, the year before the outbreak of the American Civil War, and consistently lost money until it was bought in 1883 by the Hungarian-born Joseph Pulitzer, who had immigrated to the United States in 1864. Pulitzer became a journalist and established the basis of his future fame and fortune as a publisher by buying the *St Louis Post* in 1872 and the *St Louis Dispatch* in 1878, merging them to become the *St Louis Post-Dispatch,* which is still going strong today.

Pulitzer's recipe for improving the *New York World*'s

finances was to take it firmly down market. Under his editorship, it majored on scandal, sensation and human interest stories. By the early years of the twentieth century, it was in head-to-head competition with the young William Randolph Hearst's *New York Morning Journal.* Pulitzer was forced to give up editing the paper in 1890, as he had by then gone blind, though he continued to manage the business.

The *New York World* published an eight-page comic section with its Sunday edition, called 'Fun', for which Arthur Wynne was responsible. It included puzzles, such as word squares, hidden words and joining up the dots. In the run-up to Christmas 1913, Wynne was asked to come up with a new wheeze to give 'Fun' an extra edge over the holiday season. This was how Wynne's first 'word-cross' puzzle came to be launched on the New York public.

The claim that Arthur Wynne was the 'inventor' of the modern crossword has acquired the status of historical fact, but there is no evidence that he ever made it himself. Magic squares and word squares, incorporating elements recognisable in today's crosswords, have been found in Pompeii and on ancient Egyptian monuments, dating back to the reign of the Pharaoh Rameses II (who died around 1237 BC), with inscriptions in the form of 'cross-hieroglyphs'.

The ancients aside, word puzzles and riddles, using all the tricks of the modern crossword compiler's trade, long pre-date

1913. Anagrams (taking the letters of one word or phrase to make another), rebuses (puzzles that use pictures to represent words or syllables, combined with added or deleted letters to give the answer), charades (where words or syllables are strung together to form a new word or phrase), acrostics (where letters from, say, the beginning of a series of words or lines in a poem themselves form a word or phrase), word squares (for example, 5 × 5 grids with interlocking words as solutions across and down) and cryptic definitions of words: all these existed long before Arthur Wynne was born.

Puzzles involving intersecting Across and Down words appeared in publications in the United Kingdom, the United States and elsewhere during the nineteenth century. (If the origins of the modern crossword interest you, then Roger Millington's engaging book, *The Strange World of the Crossword*, is a good starting point.) Wynne, himself, never denied that his 'word-cross' offering was based on the puzzles that he had seen in England in his youth in publications for children.

So the claim made widely for Arthur Wynne that he invented the crossword does not really stand up, since none of the essential elements of the famous 21 December 1913 puzzle was new. Equally, it is clear that the 'Fun' puzzle is light years away from the modern cryptic crossword. Judge for yourself. In the early puzzles, clues were Horizontal and Vertical, not

Across and Down. The numbering in the grid indicated where each solution began and ended.

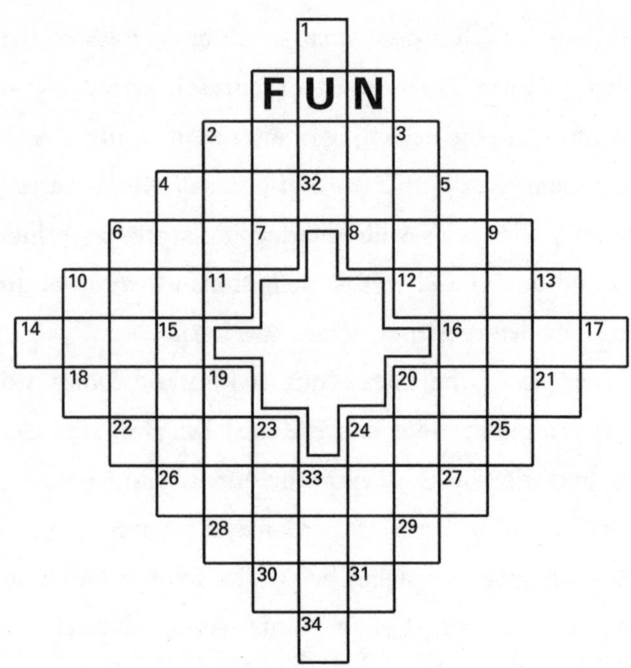

Fill in the small squares with words which agree with the following definitions:

Horizontal	Vertical
2–3. What bargain hunters enjoy.	**10–18.** The fibre of the gomuti palm.
4–5. A written acknowledgment.	**6–22.** What we all should be.
6–7. Such and nothing more.	**4–26.** A day dream.
10–11. A bird.	**2–11.** A talon.
14–15. Opposed to less.	**19–28.** A pigeon.
18–19. What this puzzle is.	**F–7.** Part of your head.
22–23. An animal of prey.	**23–30.** A river in Russia.
26–27. The close of a day.	**1–32.** To govern.
28–29. To elude.	**33–34.** An aromatic plant.
30–31. The plural of is.	**N-8.** A fist.

8–9. To cultivate.
12–13. A bar of wood or iron.
16–17. What artists learn to do.
20–21. Fastened.
24–25. Found on the seashore.

24–31. To agree with.
3–12. Part of a ship.
20–29. One.
5–27. Exchanging.
9–25. To sink in mud.
13–21. A boy.

The solution can be found at the end of this chapter.

This first Wynne puzzle has no blocked squares and the clues are not cryptic in any way. If the readers of 'Fun' knew the word for the fibre of the gomuti palm, it does not appear in any of today's standard one-volume dictionaries. His answer to 20–29 Vertical is a Scots dialect word that not many New Yorkers can have been familiar with. His synonyms for 'talon' and 'fist' are also pretty obscure and his definitions at 6–7 Horizontal and both 24–31 and 9–25 Vertical are inaccurate. It would be thought unacceptably inelegant today to have the same word appearing as a solution twice in one puzzle (10–11 Horizontal and 19–28 Vertical).

The *New York World* and its readers liked their weekly word-cross/cross-word/crossword puzzle well enough, but it did not become the rage. No other New York or American publication thought it necessary to copy the new idea. Nor did it prove to be the paper's financial salvation. Pulitzer had died in 1911 and, over the next ten years, the paper rather lost direction. It was sold to the Scripp–Howard organisation in

1930, which combined it with its *Evening Telegram* as the *New York World-Telegram*. In its final years, it became the *New York World-Telegram and Sun*, before ceasing publication entirely in 1966.

The crosswords in the *New York World*, however, did bring instant fame and fortune to two young men with an indirect Pulitzer link. They were Richard (Dick) L. Simon and M. Lincoln Schuster, who graduated from the Columbia School of Journalism in New York in 1924. (The school had opened its doors twelve years earlier as the result of a $2 million bequest to Columbia University in Pulitzer's will for the purpose of funding an institution dedicated to raising the standards of journalism.) Together the pair had decided not to go into journalism, but to try book publishing instead. To do that, though, they clearly needed a book. They approached the *New York World* with a proposal to publish a collection from the best of the puzzles that had been submitted to the paper by its readers. The outcome was a book of fifty puzzles, sold with a little pencil attached. The tyro publishers were sufficiently worried about the project to choose Plaza Publishing Company as their imprint (the name taken from their New York telephone exchange), to protect their own reputation – and credit – if the book turned out to be a complete flop. The initial print run was only 3,600 copies.

The Crossword Puzzle Book was a commercial success

beyond anyone's dreams. Retailing at $1.35 (pricey for 1924), the first printing sold out within twenty-four hours. Overnight, American newspapers from coast to coast took syndicated crosswords or commissioned their own. (The *New York Times* was one of the few to resist the new fad, only starting a Sunday crossword puzzle in 1942 and not introducing a daily one until 1950.)

Within three months the young publishers had sold 40,000 copies. A 25-cent edition was brought out. By the end of the year, sales were well over 400,000 and the duo felt confident enough to put the imprint Simon & Schuster on their third volume of puzzles. It was this financial hit that launched Simon & Schuster on its way to becoming one of the twentieth century's most successful publishing houses.

On the back of the success of the Simon & Schuster book, though he had not been responsible for producing it, Arthur Wynne persuaded a British syndicating agency, Newspaper Features, to take a batch of his puzzles. The agency succeeded in selling some of them to the *Sunday Express*. The first to be published was a small 7 × 7 grid with four pairs of blocked squares. The twenty-two clues, still called Horizontals and Verticals, were simple word definitions, such as: clue 'A coin (slang)'; solution 'BOB'. This was not the first crossword to be published in Britain; the monthly *Pearson's Magazine*, established by Arthur Pearson who also founded the *Daily Express*, had been running a regular crossword since 1922. And 1924 was not the year when the crossword craze burst on Britain. Only the *Sunday Times* immediately followed the *Sunday Express* in introducing a puzzle.

The trigger for the British craze for crosswords can be dated to 30 July 1925, when the *Daily Telegraph* became the first national daily paper to give in to what was happening on the other side of the Atlantic. The paper's original plan was to run a daily puzzle for just six weeks, until the fad had passed.

It is quite widely assumed that the first heavyweight British national daily newspaper to have given way to the new American crossword craze must have been *The Times*, because the 'Thunderer' was then very much the British Establishment's house journal and, by the mid-1930s, its crossword had become an integral part of the Establishment's lifestyle. Those who admitted to having caught the bug included the Prime Minister, Stanley Baldwin, and the Foreign Secretary, Sir Austen Chamberlain, members of the Royal Family, bishops, Sir Edward Elgar, P.G. Wodehouse and Fougasse, the cartoonist.

In fact, *The Times* held out against the new and vulgar Americanism for a further four and a half years. In the words of Adrian Bell, who set *The Times* crossword No. 1, published on 1 February 1930, those in charge at Printing House Square thought the crossword 'a toy for vacant minds'. The only thing that got them off their high editorial horses was hard evidence from the circulation department that, as a result of not having a crossword, their paper was losing sales to the *Daily Telegraph*. So worried were they about the possible hostile reaction by their core readership to such crass dumbing-down that, for a month, they ran a puzzle in the paper's weekly edition as a test marketing exercise. But this crude commercial necessity almost at once became a jewel in the paper's crown and was soon promoted as 'The World's Most Famous Crossword'.

The Times was also beaten to the draw by another internationally famous daily newspaper. On Saturday, 5 January 1929, at the top of page seven of a twenty-four-page edition, between 'Letters to the Editor' and a despatch from the paper's Berlin correspondent, the *Manchester Guardian* ran an announcement of its Competition No. 1:

> We offer two prizes – one of Two Guineas and one of One Guinea – for the best reply to an interesting and even exciting question.
>
> **If communication were established with Mars and a people found there capable of understanding messages from Earth what message (not to exceed twenty words) would you send?**

Below that, and only offering two prizes of 'One Guinea' each, came Crossword Puzzle No. 1. Solutions had to reach the paper's offices in Cross Street, Manchester, by the following Saturday. The announcement's preamble said (correctly): 'Neither of the competitions announced today will present formidable difficulties. They are designed rather to afford the reader relaxation and amusement in an easy chair, a train or a tram, than to tax all the resources alike of his intelligence and of his library.'

The *Guardian* crossword puzzle remained a weekly Saturday feature for four months, when a Wednesday puzzle was added. It did not go daily until the beginning of 1930. Today's cryptic puzzle, while still hoping to amuse, is deliberately intended to exercise the intelligence of the solver rather more than Puzzle No. 1.

Here is that first puzzle.

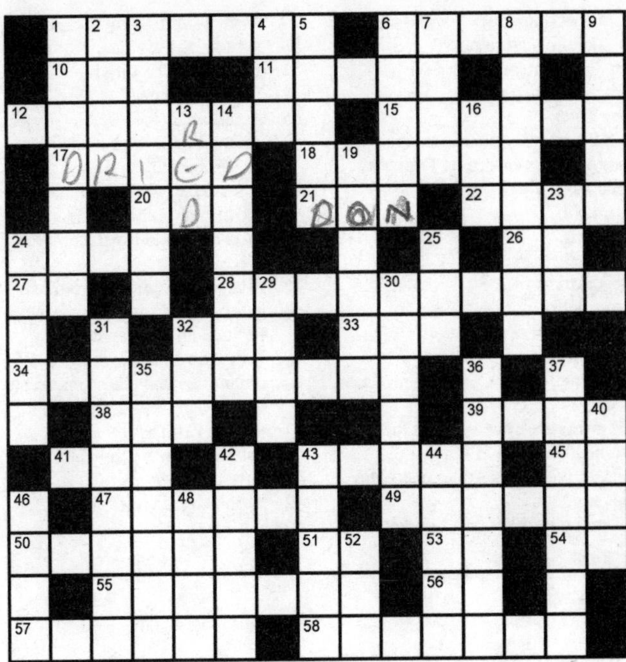

(Contains the names of several well-known politicians.)

ACROSS

1. One of our Elder Statesmen.
6. Investigation.
10. A highly taxed commodity.
11. Whatever is fast is this.
12. Glaring, but, says the dictionary, also scandalous.
15. Those who remember the Boer War will remember this statesman.
17. Wet clothes are no use until they are this.
18. Describes poetry concerned with love.
20. Some fellows call themselves this.
21. A river in Russia and a gentleman in Spain.
22. When staff is added this fish is very plain.
24. Well known in the cotton mill.
26. An important pronoun.

DOWN

1. The head of the Government.
2. Wing-shaped.
3. Military formations of the past revived in the Great War.
4. The vessel which the poet Gray called "storied."
5. Assigned fixed value to.
6. A politician as prominent in India as here.
7. Prepare a book for the press.
8. A Liberal leader.
9. A Tory ex-Chancellor.
13. Labour dislikes being called this.
14. Christopher not Joseph.
16. Part of the face.
19. One of Scott's heroines.
23. What new planets swim into.
24. Minister with historic feudal name.
25. To make one.

27. A fairly common prefix and suffix.
28. A Locarno statesman.
32. An American author.
33. Where Cain went to.
34. The Tiger.
38. A bill sometimes becomes this.
39. Instrument favoured by Orpheus.
41. Men have sought its relics in Armenia.
43. To uplift.
45. Means the same.
47. Gets tidings of.
49. Insurrection.
50. Begins a famous Miltonic sonnet.
51. A 't'-less blow.
53. Abbreviation for Canadian province.
54. Compass point.
55. An orthodox Chancellor of the Exchequer.
56. A negative in more than one Latin language.
57. A French novelist or a London editor.
58. A Labour M.P. who became a Minister and left his party.

29. A once-familiar royal name.
30. A popular novelist.
31. The reverse of timid.
32. Less than anger.
35. A politician now in the City.
36. A member of the Labour Government.
37. A financier whose name has become proverbial in the Continent.
40. Won a notable by-election for Liberalism.
42. A Liberal politician prominent before and during the war who became an ambassador.
43. Peer who gave his name to a famous committee and edited a queen's letters.
44. One of Liverpool's M.P.s.
46. One of Manchester's M.P.s.
48. Very eager.
52. Heroine of a Greek legend.

The solution can be found at the end of this chapter.

What readers of the *Manchester Guardian* got on that Saturday in 1929 bears little relation to a modern cryptic crossword. It is true that some clues, such as 20 and 22 Across, have a mildly cryptic element; but the six two-letter solutions forced some pretty unconvincing clues, particular the one for 51 Across. So even by 1930 it could not really be said that the modern cryptic crossword had arrived.

The man who truly deserves the title of the 'Father of the Modern Crossword' is the legendary Torquemada, creator of the cryptic clue. This was the pen name of Edward (Bill) Powys

Mathers. He was born at Forest Hill in London in 1892 and suffered a lifetime of seriously poor health. Perhaps as a result of this, he was a rather withdrawn and private person, but one with great enthusiasms, a thirst for esoteric knowledge and an irrepressible schoolboy sense of humour.

His efforts to join the army as an officer in 1914 failed on medical grounds, but he was accepted as a private towards the end of 1915, when casualties in France had lowered the medical pass mark for recruitment. He was, however, clearly not fit enough for the army and was discharged within a matter of months.

Powys Mathers was, rather, a man of letters, with a strong interest in poetry and things oriental. He published translations of oriental love songs and his sixteen-volume version of *The Book of the Thousand Nights and One Night* was hailed as being superior to Sir Richard Burton's. He combined all this with an addiction for detective fiction and for three years reviewed thrillers for the *Observer*.

Powys Mathers found the imported American fad to be unfulfilling, as it effectively consisted of finding the answers to incomplete and often inaccurate dictionary definitions of words. So, to amuse himself and his friends, he tried his hand at composing puzzles based on more 'cryptic' clues. His literary agent, without his permission, sold the idea to a small circulation literary magazine, the *Saturday Westminster*

Gazette, which regularly published work by the likes of D.H. Lawrence, Walter de la Mare and Rupert Brooke. The pen name that Powys Mathers adopted for these puzzles was taken from Tomás de Torquemada, the Dominican monk who was the first Spanish Inquisitor-General from 1483 to 1498, during which time he burned around 2,000 heretics.

The first twelve Torquemada puzzles, with their clues in the form of rhyming couplets, appeared in the *Saturday Westminster*, but in 1926, they transferred to the *Observer*. The first *Observer* puzzle was titled 'Feelers'; Torquemada considered he was feeling his way with his new type of clues and his new public. It was the first of a run of 670 weekly puzzles, which continued until his death in 1939 at the age of forty-six.

Torquemada built up a devoted following. But many of his clues, and often whole puzzles, were fiendish. You had to get inside his eclectic mind and see the world and language through his quirky eyes to understand his clues. For example, one of his most celebrated puzzles contained twenty-three tortured clues, each intended to produce a first name as the solution. To solve each of these clues you had to imagine two people playing the old 'Knock knock' riddle, where the first person says 'Knock knock', the second asks 'Who's there?', the first replies with a name (Mary, say), the second asks 'Mary who?' and the first delivers the punch line. In these twenty-three clues you were given the punch line and had to work out the name.

For example, you were supposed to get from '____ and a small stout (7)' to ABIGAIL by the following route:

'Knock knock.'

'Who's there?'

'Abigail.'

'Abigail who?'

'A big ale and a small stout!'

With another of these clues you were expected to work out that the correct answer from '____ropodist called about my corns? (8)' was HEZEKIAH via 'Has a chiropodist called about my corns?' If clues of this kind appeared in a *Guardian* cryptic puzzle today, there would be uproar.

In reaction to Torquemada's anarchic brilliance, a feeling grew that there should be a basic set of generally accepted rules, or at least conventions, for published cryptic crossword puzzles, so that solvers might have a fair chance of knowing that a possible solution to a clue was definitely the right one.

Three men, in particular, are associated with this next stage in the development of the cryptic puzzle. They were all schoolteachers (and all three taught the classics) at a time when grammar and exercises in syntax played a more important part in the secondary school curriculum than they do today. It is difficult not to see a connection between their day jobs and their attitude towards the pastime that made them known to a wider audience.

The first preacher of this need for greater law and order in crosswords was A.F. Ritchie, the headmaster of Wells Cathedral School and an honorary prebendary (or canon) of Wells Cathedral. In 1929 the BBC had founded the weekly *Listener* magazine, which at once established a reputation for running fiendishly difficult prize crossword puzzles. The first one received a single correct entry. The Wells headmaster soon became a star setter of these very difficult puzzles. His clues were full of classical and biblical references. He took as his pen name Afrit (A.F. RITchie), a powerful demon of Arabian mythology.

Afrit's thoughts on what did and did not constitute a fair cryptic clue were most fully set out in the short introduction he wrote to his collection of *Armchair Crosswords*, published in 1949. In it he also made reference to a definitive, as yet unwritten *Book of the Crossword*, an 'exhaustive treatise' on the subject, which would lay this injunction (printed in bold type) on the crossword compiler:

> **I need not mean what I say, but I must say what I mean.**

This epigrammatic play on the well-known exchange in *Alice in Wonderland* – March Hare: 'Then you should say what you mean'; Alice: 'I do, at least – at least I mean what I say – that's the same thing, you know' – has become the 'golden rule' of the modern cryptic crossword. It means that the cryptic clue, read as a whole, can be – indeed, is expected to be – misleading. But, when deconstructed into its component parts, the clue must also fairly lead any educated solver to what is clearly the only possible right answer.

Prebendary Ritchie died in harness in 1954 without ever having had the time to write his *Book of the Crossword.* That task was taken on by the man who became Torquemada's successor at the *Observer*: Derrick Somerset Macnutt. On Torquemada's death, Macnutt set a puzzle containing (unclued) the words of a quatrain paying tribute to the skills of the great man. (This was a puzzle form that Torquemada had himself often used.) It was published and D.S. Macnutt then asked if there was a position vacant at the *Observer.* Initially offered a job-share with two others, in 1945 he became the paper's sole crossword editor.

D.S. Macnutt's first pen name as a setter was Tesremos, his middle name reversed. But by 1945 he had adopted the pen name Ximenes, the anglicisation of the first name of Jiménez de Cisneros, the Spanish cardinal and grand inquisitor for Castile and Léon between 1507 and 1517.

Macnutt was a housemaster and head of Classics at Christ's Hospital school in Sussex. At the start of his setting career he was an unquestioning admirer of Torquemada (as shown by his choice of another grand inquisitor for his pen name), but he soon fell in with Afrit's view that the business needed a generally accepted road map and contributed the foreword to *Armchair Crosswords.* His *Book of the Crossword* finally appeared in 1966 as *Ximenes on the Art of the Crossword,* written in collaboration with the third of our trio, Alec Robins.

Alec Robins was Manchester born and bred, and educated at Manchester Grammar School and Manchester University. He became seriously interested in crosswords during the nearly three years he spent in a TB sanatorium in Norfolk, having returned to England with the disease in 1945 after serving with the Royal Corps of Signals in India and Ceylon for four years. He became head of Classics at Chorlton Grammar School for boys in Manchester and, when that closed, moved to Strand Grammar School for girls in the late 1960s. For many years, Alec Robins contributed puzzles to *Competitors Journal,* which later merged into *John Bull,* and also to *Computer Weekly,* which is now part of Reed Business Press. But he made his reputation with the many innovative puzzles he set, as Zander, for the *Listener* and for his Everyman puzzles in the *Observer,* which he set for each alternate month for thirty-three years. He also set for *The Times* in the 1990s. In the *Guardian* he was Custos, implying that he saw himself as something of a custodian of proper standards, though he was far too kindly and gentle to be in any way an authoritarian figure. His own book, *Teach Yourself Crosswords,* first published in 1975, had an enormous influence on a whole generation of crossword setters. He died, aged eighty, in 1998.

The Macnutt/Robins approach to bringing order to the world of cryptic clues is summarised in the first chapter of *Ximenes on the Art of the Crossword*:

> . . . the purpose of this book . . . is the ambitious one – perhaps too ambitious – of trying to arrive at a system of principles which can make the crossword more enjoyable and rewarding to solvers, whether they be among the millions of desultory solvers, content sometimes to fill in only part of a puzzle to pass an odd half-hour, or among the many thousands of real enthusiasts, determined to reach a full solution, whether of an easy or a difficult puzzle.

The aim was to move towards a universal grammar for all setters of all crossword puzzles, be they easy or next to impossible, which would give all solvers the same starting point. The writings of D.S. Macnutt and Alec Robins resulted in a widespread acceptance by crossword setters and editors of a common set of conventions as to what constituted a fair clue. This led to a new adjective, Ximenean.

For the past forty years Ximenean rules have been the dominant influence on the setting of cryptic crosswords in this country. The next chapter sets out how they work in practice.

But they were not carved in stone and the development of crossword language and conventions is a continuous process. At the *Guardian*, Araucaria in particular has pushed the boundaries of cluemanship beyond the limits that a rigid Ximenean would accept and has given much pleasure in doing so. Of the younger *Guardian* setters, Paul and Enigmatist have followed enthusiastically in his wake. And there have been other important figures in the story of how we got to where we are today, like Edmund Akenhead, *The Times*'s crossword editor from 1965 to 1983, and Jonathan Crowther, who succeeded Ximenes as a crossword setter for the *Observer* in 1972 and who has set the weekly Azed puzzle for that paper ever since. (His pen name, incidentally, is the reverse of that of another Grand Inquisitor, Don Diego del Deza, Archbishop of Seville, whose official score of heretics burned alive during his term of office between 1498 and 1507 was 2,592.)

Considering the central place that the cryptic crossword now enjoys in British newspapers and magazines, its history has been surprisingly short. The giants in the story, Torquemada apart, are all post-war figures. The modern conventions only began to gain currency after 1949 and were only codified for the first time in 1966. Seen in that perspective, the cryptic crossword is still in its prime of youth.

Solution to Arthur Wynne's 'Fun' puzzle

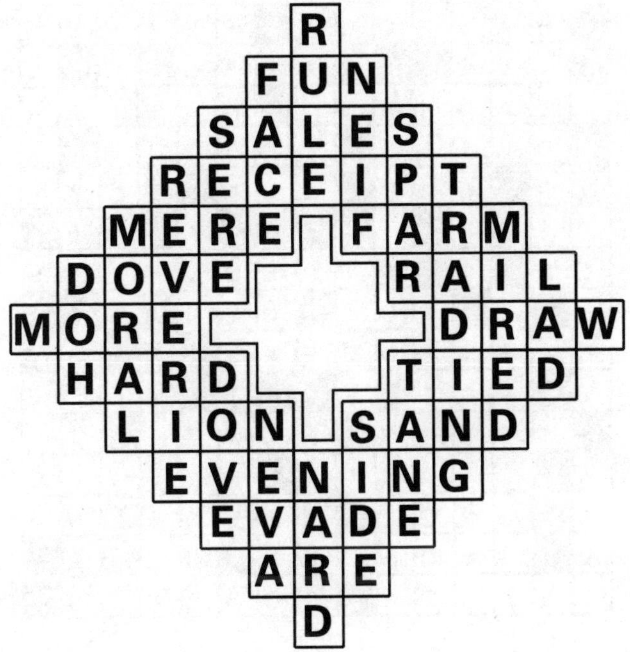

Solution to the *Guardian* Crossword Puzzle No. 1

■	1 B	2 A	3 L	F	O	4 U	5 R	■	6 S	7 E	A	8 R	C	9 H
■	10 A	L	E	■	■	11 R	A	P	I	D	■	U	■	O
12 F	L	A	G	13 R	14 A	N	T	■	15 M	I	16 L	N	E	R
■	17 D	R	I	E	D	■	18 E	19 R	O	T	I	C	■	N
■	W	■	20 O	D	D	■	21 D	O	N	■	22 P	I	23 K	E
24 P	I	R	N	■	I	■	■	W	■	25 W	■	26 M	E	■
27 E	N	■	S	■	28 S	29 T	R	E	30 S	E	M	A	N	N
R	■	31 F	■	32 P	O	E	■	33 N	O	D	■	N	■	■
34 C	L	E	35 M	E	N	C	E	A	U	■	36 S	■	37 S	■
Y	■	38 A	C	T	■	K	■	■	T	■	39 L	U	T	40 E
■	41 A	R	K	■	42 C	■	43 E	L	A	44 T	E	■	45 I	D
46 N	■	47 L	E	48 A	R	N	S	■	49 R	I	S	I	N	G
50 A	V	E	N	G	E	■	51 H	52 I	■	53 N	S	■	54 N	E
L	■	55 S	N	O	W	D	E	N	■	56 N	E	■	E	■
57 L	E	S	A	G	E	■	58 R	O	B	E	R	T	S	■

Two

Breaking the code

The starting point with a cryptic puzzle is to understand that the correct solution to a clue is not the one that the actual words of the clue seem to suggest. Hence, 'cryptic'.

In a Quick crossword the answers to the clues are straightforward. For example, the answer to 'Blue flower (6)' might be VIOLET or ZINNIA. In a cryptic crossword, you know that neither of these can be right. The 'Blue flower (6)' will not be something that grows, but something that flows and happens to go with 'blue'. So the answer will be DANUBE. (If the clue had been 'Blue flower (4)' and not 'Blue flower (6)', the answer, as like as not, would be NILE.

The next point is that the standard cryptic clue is made up of two basic elements. The first element is some kind of definition of the required answer and the second is a cryptic code for getting there. Normally, the definition will be either at the beginning or the end of the clue, not in the middle.

The definition

The first stage towards solving a clue in a cryptic puzzle is trying to identify which part of the wording of the clue gives you the definition of the solution. To a beginner, this is not an easy process. In addition, it is part of the art of the crossword setter to write clues that camouflage the definition. It will get easier with practice as you begin to recognise the tricks that setters get up to with words, but essentially you start by looking at the beginning and end of the clue and guessing where the definition might be hidden.

The game gets easier, of course, once you have solved the first clue, because you then have intersecting letters to help you with other clues. In fact, with letters from the intersecting answers to other clues already filled into the grid, a likely word that fits the space for another solution may jump out at you and you can then look to see whether any part of the clue is a definition of that word. You would, in this case, be starting to solve the clue backwards, from the answer to the clue, rather than from the clue to the answer. If, though, you can see a word that fits with already existing letters in the numbered space for a particular solution and if you can see that part of the clue provides a definition for that word, then you can be pretty certain that you are on the right track.

We are dealing at this first stage just with the **definition** element of a clue. In the second part of this chapter you will meet all the **cryptic** devices that setters use, which you need to decode in order to find the solution to a clue. Let us start with five examples just to see how the **definition** of a solution is concealed in a clue. Each clue will appear again when we come to look at how various types of cryptic device can be decoded.

Charlemagne then embraces one that's attractive (6) [Taupi]

Look for a possible definition either at the 'Charlemagne' or at the 'attractive' end of the clue. If you have no cross-checking letters already filled in to help you, the answer may not be obvious. But, if you have already got M_ _ _E_ (or, better still, M_G_E_), it might strike you that the solution could be MAGNET (something that attracts), because you cannot think of any six-letter word beginning with M that has anything to do with the Holy Roman Emperor. So, in this first example, the definition was at the end of the clue.

Here is one where it is at the beginning:

Foreign cops seem grand, if disorganised (9) [Gordius]

The definition is 'Foreign cops' and, if you already had the letters G_N_A_M_S from other clues, you might correctly guess that the answer is GENDARMES.

With the next clue, the definition is again at the beginning:

Sort of butter made from vegetable and fruit (6) [Rufus]

Even without existing letters as clues, you might guess that the right answer is PEANUT (since peanut butter is a sort of butter). If you already had the first P entered in the grid, getting there would be even quicker.

The setter may well try to make the detective work involved in this first stage into more of a challenge by giving the definition itself in a cryptic code. For example:

Sting, for example, animal, then girl, then me (5,4) [Paul]

is an indirect, rather than a direct, definition for the answer, as 'Sting' is an example of a STAGE NAME and

Eleven city cars (9,6) [Janus]

uses 'eleven' in the sense of a (football) team as a definition of BLACKBURN ROVERS.

Unusual definitions

What has been said so far holds for 'normal' cryptic clues. But there are two particular kinds of cryptic clue that depart from the norm. The first is known as **double definition** and the second as **& lit**.

With double definitions, as the term implies, the clue consists not of one part definition and one part cryptic indicator, but simply of two definitions linked together, each leading to the same answer. A simple example of such a clue would be:

Beef or grouse (8)

Since this clue is appearing in a cryptic crossword, the answer is not going to be anything to do with meat or a game bird. Here beef and grouse are not nouns, but verbs – both (a double definition) meaning to COMPLAIN.

There are, as you would expect, variations of the double definition clue. 'Run outside! (5)' [Bunthorne] is an example of a double definition clue for EXTRA, where the solution itself has two meanings (as a noun, an extra is a run in cricket and, as an adjective, it means 'additional' i.e. outside). The clue 'Burden of wood? (6)' [Araucaria] for the solution LUMBER is both the verb to encumber and the generic noun for wood. In the same way, 'Release without charge (4)' or 'Available for love (4)' could both be double definition clues for FREE (free = release, without charge, available, for love).

The two parts of a double definition clue can themselves also be cryptic in character. Thus 'Is Rupert Murdoch old-fashioned? (6,3,5)' [Chifonie] gives you a double definition for BEHIND THE TIMES, where the first part is a cryptic reference to the fact the Murdoch owns *The Times* and the second part is a simple definition of old-fashioned.

Such clues do not have to confine themselves to being just double definitions. 'Carp, grouse and beef (8)' would be a three-course banquet leading to COMPLAIN. In *On the Art of the Crossword*, Ximenes used 'That's a deal! Swindled, proper (4)' as a triple definition clue for DONE.

The second special category of clue, **& lit** (meaning 'and literally'), is where the whole wording of the clue – not just part of it – 'literally' provides a definition of the answer. It is a favourite device of many setters, because it can produce some elegant clues.

As with the previous examples, the 'cryptic' devices used in these clues will be explained later in this chapter. They are given here just to show how **& lit** clues work – with the whole clue providing the definition of the required answer:

Many set free (7) [Custos]

AMNESTY

Somewhat discourteous language (5) [Chifonie]

SLANG

Key words (4,6) [Gordius]

OPEN SESAME

He isn't all there (7) [Shed]

AMPUTEE

Bar of soap (3,6,6) [Rufus]

THE ROVER'S RETURN

A stiff examination (10) [Custos]

POSTMORTEM

The cryptic codes

Having seen that the definition part of a cryptic clue is to be found at the beginning or the end (except in the **double/ multiple definition** and the **& lit** cases), we can now move on to the various types of cryptic devices that setters use.

It is not fruitful, or even possible, to try to provide a complete catalogue of all the rules for cryptic clues, as Ximenes and Alec Robins bravely set out to do. This is because the cryptic crossword is constantly evolving and setters are always trying to push the boundaries forward, or to find variations and mutations of existing forms. What crossword editors accept as a fair clue is, as a result, gradually changing all the time, as solvers come to accept some new convention as being fair.

The intention of this book, aimed at beginners, is simply to describe and give examples of the main types of clues currently being deployed. Armed with this intelligence, you will find that you can understand the basic mental and linguistic processes of the setters and so solve some or most of their clues. After that, you will be able to cope with new fashions and recognise individual setters' little ways on your own.

Charades

As with the parlour game, where one side acts out each syllable of the word that has to be guessed, these clues build up the required answer, bit by bit. Here are some examples, several already encountered in the discussion of definitions.

Excluded and finished in every respect (3,3,3) [Quantum]
Definition: 'in every respect' = OUT AND OUT
Components: excluded = out, finished = out

Sort of butter made from vegetable and fruit (6) [Rufus]

Definition: 'Sort of butter' = PEANUT

Components: vegetable = pea, fruit = nut

Sting, for example, animal, then girl, then me (5,4) [Paul]

Definition: 'Sting, for example' = STAGE NAME

Components: animal = stag, girl = Ena, + me (STAG/E NA/ME)

Eleven city cars (9,6) [Janus]

Definition: 'Eleven' = BLACKBURN ROVERS

Components: city = Blackburn, cars = Rovers

Beastly male commanded individual to work hard (6,4) [Pasquale]

Definition: 'work hard' = BUCKLE DOWN

Components: beastly male = buck, commanded = led, individual = own (BUCK/LE D/OWN)

Anagrams

In these clues something will tell you that the individual letters contained in a word or phrase must be rearranged to form another word or phrase. There are no fixed rules about what that something can be and setters try hard to avoid using an **anagram indicator** that sticks out like a sore thumb, thus making the solution too obvious. So, when you first scan a clue to guess where the definition is likely to be found, part of your mind should also be alert to the possibility that the wording of the clue may indicate that there is an anagram about. Any suspicion that this may be the case can be tested by checking the letter count given at the end of the clue against the number of letters in the word or words that might be candidates as **anagram fodder**.

Here are some examples of clues involving anagrams:

Foreign cops seem grand, if disorganised (9) [Gordius]
Definition: 'Foreign cops' = GENDARMES
Components: anagram indicator 'if disorganised', anagram fodder 'seem grand'

Proverbial aphrodisiac bees can produce (7) [Araucaria]
Definition: 'Proverbial aphrodisiac' = ABSENCE (as in 'absence makes the heart grow fonder')
Components: anagram indicator 'produce', anagram fodder 'bees can'

Compile faulty argument (7) [Chifonie]
Definition: 'argument' = POLEMIC
Components: anagram indicator 'faulty', anagram fodder 'compile'

Cruel twist, a source of pain (5) [Auster]

Definition: 'A source of pain' = ULCER

Components: anagram indicator 'twist', anagram fodder 'cruel'

Were they ruffled after she dressed? (8) [Rover]

Definition: Were they ruffled? = FEATHERS

Components: anagram indicator 'dressed', anagram fodder 'after she'

The above clue for FEATHERS ended with a question mark for the normal reason that the clue is in the form of a question. But punctuation can also be used as part of a clue's cryptic code. We shall discuss cryptic punctuation, including the non-normal use of question marks, in the next chapter, starting on page 90.

Hidden clues

Something in one of these clues will hint that the letters of the solution are to be found running consecutively elsewhere in that clue. This is usually quite easy to spot, as it is hard to include a hint that is both fair and well disguised. Such clues become even easier to solve if you have managed to fill in one or more of the cross-checking letters from other clues. Most puzzles contain one such clue (or even two), but no more.

Anagram indicators

An anagram indicator is any word or words in a clue that tell you that you need to make an anagram. This list is just an indication of the sort of words that you should be looking out for.

abnormal
about
adapted
addled
adjusted
adrift
afresh
after a fashion
agitated
all over the place
alter(ed)
amiss
anew
anyhow
around
arrange(d)
askew
assembly
assortment
at odds
at sea
awkward(ly)
awry

bad(ly)
bastard
beaten (up)
become
bend/bent
bizarre
blend(ed)
boil(ed)
break/broken
brew
broadcast
building
by arrangement
by mistake

can be
careless(ly)
causes
change(d)
chaos
characters
chop(ped up)
circulate(d)
cocktail
complicate(d)
components
compose(d of)
compound
comprise
confuse(d)
constituents
construct
convert(ed/ible)
cook(ed)
correct(ed)
corrupt(ed)
could be
crack(ed)
crazy
criminal
cunningly
curious(ly)

damage(d)
dance/dancing
dealt with
deform(ed)
demolished
deploy(ed)
derived from
design(ed)
develop(ed)
deviation
dicky
different(ly)
disarray
disfigure(d)
disguise(d)
dishevelled
dislocation
dismantled
disorder(ed/ly)
dispersed
disposed (of)
disruption
disseminated
distressed
disturbance
diversified

dizzy
doctor(ed)
dreadful(ly)
dressed
drunk
dud

eccentric(ally)
edit(ed)
engendering
ensemble
entangle(d)
erratic(ally)
erupting
essentials
excited
exotic
explode(d)
extraordinarily

fabricate(d)
false
fancy/fanciful
fantastic
fashion(ed/ing)
faulty
fermented
fiddle(d)
figuring in
find
fluid
flurried
foolish(ly)
for a change
forced
forge(d)
form (of)
fractured
fragments
free(ly)
fresh(ly)
frolicking
fudge
funny (looking)

garbled
gets
gives (rise to)
ground

haphazard
hash
havoc
haywire
hide
higgledy-piggledy

ill
ill-disposed/formed/treated
improper(ly)
in a ferment/jumble/mess/whirl
incorrect(ly)
in disarray/ disguise/error/ruins etc
inducing
ingredients
interfered with
involve(d)
irregular(ly/ity)

jittery
juggled
jumbled
jumping
kind of
kinky

letters of/from
loose(ly)
lunatic

mad(ly)
made (from/of/up)
make-up
mal-formed/function/treated)
managed
mangled
manoeuvre
mash
maybe
medley
mess
minced
mis-handle/shapen/take/use)
mix(ed/ture)
modelled
modified
moving
muddle(d)
mutilated
mutinous(ly)

naughty
new
newly made/formed
not properly/right/straight/in order
novel

odd

off
order(ed/ly)
organise(d)
original(ly)
otherwise
out (of joint/sorts)

peculiar
perhaps
perverse(ly)
pervert(ed)
phoney
pie
plastic
play(ing tricks)
poor(ly)
possible/possibly
potential(ly)
prepare(d)
problem
processing
produce
production
pseudo
put out/right/
straight

ragged
rambling
random(ly)
recollected
rectified
reeling
reformed
regulated
repaired
replaced
reveal(ed)
review(ed)
revolting
revolutionary
rigged
riot(ing/ous)
rock(ing/y)
rotten
roughly
ruin(ed/ous)
rum
run(ning)
rupture(d)

sad(ly)
scatter(ed)
set off/out
shake(n)
shambles
shift(ed/ing)
silly
sloppy
smash(ed/ing)
somehow
spill(ed)
spin(ning)
spoil(t)
stagger(ed)
stew
strange(ly)
substitute(d)
surprising(ly)
suspect
swirl(ing)
switch(ed)

tangled
tattered
tidied (up)
tipsy
tortuous(ly)
train(ed)
transform(ation/ed)
translate(d)
treat(ed/ment)
tricky
trouble(d)
tumbling
turn(ed)
twist(ed/er)

undone
unnatural
unrestrained
unruly
unsettle(d)
unsteady
untidy
unusual(ly)
upheaval
upset
used

vague
varied
version (of)
volatile

wander(ing)
warp(ed)
wayward
weave/woven
weird
wild
worried
wrecked
writhing

Here are some examples:

Charlemagne then embraces one that's attractive (6) [Taupi]

Definition: 'one that's attractive' = MAGNET

Components: the hidden clue indicator is 'embraces'

charleMAGNE Then

London Eye component – in climbing on, do laugh! (7) [Brummie]

Definition: 'London Eye component' = GONDOLA

Components: the hidden clue indicator is 'in'

climbinG ON DO LAugh

Next race yields a bonus (5) [Beale]

Definition: 'a bonus' = EXTRA

Components: the hidden clue indicator is 'yields'

nEXT RAce

Some sunlit Chinese fruit (6) [Rover]

Definition: 'fruit' = LITCHI

Components: the hidden indicator is 'Some'

sunLIT CHInese

Government wants some more pub licences (8) [Hazard]

Definition: 'Government' = REPUBLIC

Components: the hidden indicator is 'some'

moRE PUB LICences

Hidden clue indicators

These are the kind of words and phrases that warn you to look out for strings of letters that may form part of the required solution.

a bit/part/piece/section of
a little

by no means all

carried/contained by/in
content(s) of

found in
from

gripped by

held by/in
holding

imprisoned by
in

not all

only a little/part/piece of

partially

some
stuffed into

taken from

within
wrapped (up) in

Split words

Here, to reach the right answer, something from the cryptic part of the clue's solution has to be put inside or outside something else. The clue will also contain an indicator as to which part goes inside and/or outside.

Here are some examples:

Wild time in Florida (5) [Gordius]
Definition: 'Wild' = FERAL
Components: the indicator 'in' shows that a word for 'time' has to divide 'Florida'; time = era, FL is an abbreviation for Florida
F<ERA>L

(Abbreviations commonly used in cryptic crosswords are discussed in the next chapter.)

Rascal commandeers transport to leave bivouac (6,4) [Chifonie]
Definition: 'leave bivouac' = STRIKE CAMP
Components: The indicator is 'commandeers', i.e. a word for 'rascal' seizes a word for some kind of 'transport'; rascal = scamp, transport = trike
S<TRIKE> CAMP

Look for water, finding measure about a quarter (5) [Paul]
Definition: 'Look for water' = DOWSE
Components: the indicator 'about' invites a word for 'measure' to be put round 'a quarter'; measure = dose, a (compass) quarter = W (as in N,S,E & W)
DO<W>SE

Swimmer about to go in, then rest (8) [Moley]

Definition: 'rest' = BREATHER

Components: the indicator 'to go in' invites a word for 'about' to split another word for 'swimmer', swimmer = bather, about = re

B<RE>ATHER

Snail, with flower circle, quietly accepted by deity (10) [Audreus]

Definition: 'Snail' = GASTEROPOD

Components: the indicator 'accepted' shows that words or letters for 'flower, circle and quietly' need to split a word for 'deity'; flower = aster, circle = O, quietly = p(iano), deity = god

G<ASTER/O/P>OD

Split word indicators

These are the kind of words and phrases to warn you that, in the solution, something has to go inside or outside something else. The basic word may come in a variety of forms, depending on the context of the clue e.g. absorb, absorbs, absorbed, absorbing.

Outside

about	assimilate	clutch
absorb		confine
accept	capture	contain
admit	carry	cut by

divide by
drink
during

embrace
encircle
enclose
engulf
entrap
exterior to

fill by
frame

get about/around
grab
grip

harbour
hold
house

impound
imprison
include
incorporate
interrupt by
involve

keep

occupy by
outside

part by
pocket

receive
retain
ring

separate by
set about
shelter
split by
surround
swallow

take in
trap

without
wrap

Inside

absorbed/accepted/ accommodated by

beset by

captured/carried/ clutched/confined by/in
content(s) (of)
cut

divide
drunk/eaten by

embraced/encircled/ entrapped by/in
enclosure
enter

filling
frame by/in

go in
grabbed by

harboured/housed by/in

imprisoned/ impounded/ incorporated by/in
in . . .
inside
interrupt
intervene/involve in

line

occupy

part
pocketed by
put into

received/retained by/in

separate
set in
sheltered by
split
stuff
surrounded/ swallowed by

taken in by
trapped by/in
tucked into

within
wrapped in

Reversals

These clues will contain an indicator that a solution (or part of it) will be made up of a word or letters written backwards (or, for Down clues, upwards).

Here are some examples of reversals:

Australian bird stood everyone up (7) [Bonxie]

Definition: 'Australian bird' = ROSELLA (an Australian parrot)

Components: the indicator (in this case for a Down clue) is 'up'; stood = rose, everyone = all

ROSE/ALL (rev)

Composer's weight in car going back (6) [Araucaria]

Definition: 'Composer' = MOZART

Components: the indicator is 'going back', showing that a 'weight' needs to split a reversal of a kind of 'car'; weight = oz (i.e. ounce), car = tram

TRA<OZ>M(rev)

Quick to return to sin (4) [Janus]

Definition: 'Sin' = EVIL

Components: the indicator 'to return' indicates a reversal of a word meaning 'quick'; quick = live (as opposed to dead)

LIVE (rev)

I wander around as antipodean (5) [Paul]

Definition: 'antipodean' = MAORI

Components: the indicator 'around' tells you that a phrase meaning 'I wander' needs to be reversed; wander = roam

I/ROAM (all rev)

Fat Ida turns up to model (7) [Don Putnam]

Definition: 'Fat' = ADIPOSE

Components: the indicator 'turns up' means that 'Ida' needs to be reversed and added to a word for 'model'; model = pose

IDA(rev)/POSE

Reversal indicators

These are the kind of words and phrases that warn you that something in the clue or in the solution is written backwards.

Across and Down

alternative(ly)
back(ed/wards/ to front)
brought/given/going /sent back
echoing

in recession/retreat/ retrospect
on reflection
overturned
reflective(ly)
retired/retiring
retrograde
retroversion

return(ed)
reversal/reversed
set back
taken aback
the alternative/ other/wrong way
turn(ed) (back/over)

Across only

(coming) from the East

Down only

ascendant/ascending
brought up
climbing
elevated/elevation
giving rise to/up
invert(ed)
mount(ed/ing)
not written down
raised/rising
sent/set/shown/
turned up
up(bringing/lifted/set/side-down/wards)
uppish
write/written up

Pluses, minuses and switches

Sometimes the wording of a clue will indicate that some letters in a word need to be added, or taken away, or somehow switched.

For example:

Criminal gets in at the back of the house (7) [Rufus]

Definition: 'Criminal' = VILLAIN

Components: house = villa, with 'in' added to the end

VILLA/IN

Cheeky and careless, but not initially rash (8) [Arachne]

Definition: 'Cheeky' = IMPUDENT

Components: careless = imprudent, 'but not' indicates that

something should be removed, 'initially rash' = r

IMP(r)UDENT

Tunnel regularly shocking, off limits (8) [Paul]

Definition: 'off limits' = UNLAWFUL

Components: 'regularly' indicates that you have to take alternate letters of 'tunnel', shocking = awful

(t)U(n)N(e)L/AWFUL

Smoke volume cut out by force in the island (6) [Gordius]

Definition: 'island' = TOBAGO

Components: smoke = tobacco, volume = cc (i.e. centilitre), force = g (i.e. gravity), 'cut out by' indicates that volume is to be switched for force

TOBA(cc/G)O

Bridges often are in real need of water, lacking power (6) [Brummie]

Definition: 'Bridges often are' = ARCHED

Components: 'in real need of water' = parched, 'lacking' indicates that a subtraction is involved, power = p

(p)ARCHED

Initial letters

In these clues there is an indication that all or part of the answer is made up of the initial letters from a string of words in the clue. These are usually some of the easier clues to spot, because the range of indicator words available for them is limited ('heads', 'initially' or 'initials', 'starts' or 'to start with', 'beginnings', 'openings' and 'firsts' are the ones that you will most commonly meet).

Here are some examples:

Not every good European voter heads for the desert (5)
[Bunthorne]

Definition: 'desert'= NEGEV

Indicator: 'heads'

Components: N(ot) e(very) g(ood) E(uropean) v(oter)

College heads from Oxford, readers in English literature (5)
[Quantum]

Definition: 'College' = ORIEL (the Oxford College)

Indicator: 'heads from'

Components: O(xford) r(eaders) i(n) E(nglish) l(iterature)

New gaffer initially interrupts foremost film director (9)
[Chifonie]

Definition: 'film director' = PREMINGER

Indicators: ‘initially’ for initial letters, ‘interrupts’ for a split word

Components: N(ew) g(affer) splitting a word for ‘foremost’ = premier

PREMI<NG>ER

Course record set outside Munich, initially (5) [Troll]

Definition: ‘Course’ = EPSOM (the racecourse)

Indicator: ‘initially’

Components: record = EP (the old five-track single), s(et) o(utside) M(unich)

EP/S/O/M

The countryman’s asparagus starts to grow ripe and sweet when birds are around (12) [Rover]

Definition: ‘The countryman’s asparagus’ = SPARROWGRASS (a dialect word)

Indicators: ‘starts to’ for initial letters; ‘are around’ for a split word

Components: g(row) r(ipe) a(nd) s(weet) splitting a word for ‘birds’ = sparrows

SPARROW<G/R/A/S>S

Homophones and puns

Clues often use homophones (words that sound the same, but are spelled differently and have quite different meanings): for example, bear and bare, hair and hare. They can also make play with words that are spelled the same but can be pronounced in more than one way and then mean something quite different: for example, object (a thing, or to make an objection), or sewer (someone who sews, or a drain). These clues will contain some wording (for example, 'they say', 'on air' or 'it's said') to indicate that there is a homophone about, either in the clue or in the solution.

The most frequently used example of a word which can be pronounced in two different ways, producing two different meanings, is 'flower', which can be something that blooms or something that flows, i.e. a river. In this case both pronunciations produce nouns, but often one will produce a noun and another a verb or adjective. For example, 'refuse' pronounced as a noun is garbage, but pronounced as a verb means to say no.

The deceptive characteristic of these words gives setters endless possibilities for writing clues that send you off in quite the wrong direction, so you need to be particularly on the lookout for them. There are hundreds of such words that can be pronounced in more than one way, becoming different parts of speech and acquiring quite different meanings in the process. Here is a sample of the kind of word you need to look out for: August, bass, bow, close, defect, detail, entrance, hinder, incense, lead, live, number, project, putter, row, supply, tarry, tear, wind and worsted.

Here are some examples of clues involving homophones:

How brawls might sound put into words (6) [Brummie]
Definition: 'put into words' = PHRASE / frays

Compelled to hear the female servant (4) [Janus]
Definition: 'Compelled' = MADE / maid

Run-down sound of recording device (5) [Taupi]
Definition: 'Run-down' = SEEDY / CD

Report of infliction of pain on arsonist? (7) [Araucaria]
Definition: 'arsonist' = TORCHER / torture

Marine beast's audible cry (4) [Troll]
Definition: 'cry' = WAIL / whale

& lit

We have now run through eight different types of cryptic device that setters use in their clues. But you will remember from the introduction to **definitions** at the beginning of this chapter that there is one special category of clue, the **& lit**. With these clues, the whole wording provides the definition, but at the same time the whole wording contains the cryptic coding. This can be one or a combination of any of the devices that we have examined in this chapter, or the whole wording can itself be cryptic. Here are examples to illustrate the range:

Many set free (7) [Custos] = AMNESTY
Anagram of 'many set' indicated by 'free'

Somewhat discourteous language (5) [Chifonie] = SLANG
Hidden clue indicated by 'somewhat'
(discourteouS LANGuage)

For him to laze is unusual (6) [Rufus] = ZEALOT
Anagram of 'to laze' indicated by 'is unusual'

Amundsen's forwarding address (4) [Bunthorne] = MUSH
The whole clue is cryptic, based on the word of command that the Norwegian explorer, Roald Amundsen, shouted to get his huskies pulling

Key words (4,6) [Gordius] = OPEN SESAME
The whole clue is cryptic, these being the words used by Ali Baba to open the door of the den of thieves

Some other tricks of the trade

Although there can never be a definitive catalogue of the tricks setters get up to in their efforts to baffle and entertain, the cryptic devices listed above are the ones that you will regularly encounter.

You will also, however, run into other tricks as well as variations of the main ones. Spotting them simply requires a rather cynical approach to the apparent meaning of words. It is an attitude of mind, not any special intelligence, that marks the difference between the Quick and the Cryptic solver.

To help you in the process of acquiring that attitude of mind, here is a selection of some of the other kinds of codes that setters deploy from time to time. If you can spot these when you see them, you will soon be able to spot others, old and new.

Typographical clues

These clues use letters, numbers, symbols and spacing as their cryptic element.

For example:

Cat
Cat
Cat (5-4,4) [Paul] = THREE-LINE WHIP

(a cat-o'-nine-tails or cat is a whip, written here on three lines to produce a 'three-line whip', the most serious kind of instruction on how to vote in the Houses of Parliament)

50% off (4-6) [Rufus] = HALF-ASLEEP
(you are 100 per cent asleep when you have nodded off)

? (1,6,1,4) [Orlando] = I HAVEN'T A CLUE

Spoonerisms

The Reverend W.A. Spooner, Warden of New College, Oxford, who died in 1930, famously muddled the beginnings of words when speaking. Thus, for example, his 'half-formed wish' became a 'half-warmed fish'. Some setters make use of his affliction in their clues.

Here are three typical examples:

Refuse to go here with Spooner's broken racket (7) [Araucaria]
Definition: 'Refuse to go here' = DUSTBIN
Components: a Spoonerism of 'bust din', i.e. broken = BUST, racket = DIN

Spooner's resentful listener is an antisocial character (9) [Shed]
Definition: 'an antisocial character' = LITTERBUG
Components: a Spoonerism of 'bitter lug', i.e. resentful =

BITTER, listener = LUG (slang for an ear)

Silent film star's scene at Little Bighorn, as delivered by Spooner (6,6) [Paul]

Definition: 'Silent film star' = BUSTER KEATON

Components: a spoonerism of 'Custer beaten', i.e. a reference to the US cavalry's General Custer, who was defeated and killed by Sioux Indians in 1876 at Little Bighorn, Montana

Regional accents and rhyming slang

In real life, cockneys seem to use remarkably little rhyming slang these days, if they ever did. But this does not in any way inhibit crossword setters in writing clues. They also make free use of regional accents, particularly from Scotland, Ireland, the north of England and the East End of London.

Here are examples of this genre:

Menace of the Krays brings worry (4) [Paul]

Definition: 'worry' = FRET

Components: menace = threat, which the Kray brothers might have pronounced as 'fret'

Place noted for its fair hair (6) [Rover]

Definition: 'Place noted for its fair' = BARNET

Components: Barnet Fair = 'hair' in rhyming slang

Trouble from 'orrible weather (3) [Chifonie]

Definition: 'Trouble' (as a verb) = AIL, as in 'Oh what can ail thee, Knight at arms' (Keats)

Component: Horrible weather = HAIL, from which the 'h' needs to be dropped

Personification

These clues are written as if an object were a person. Setters also quite often refer to themselves (or their *Guardian* pen names) in clues ('I' or 'me', for example, could indicate SHED and 'setter's' could indicate MINE). They also refer to 'the *Guardian*' as 'us' and to *Guardian* solvers as 'you' (or sometimes, archaically, as 'ye').

Here are some examples:

I won't cross the line to give the fellow a beating (7) [Enigmatist]

Definition: 'I won't cross the line' = TANGENT (a line that only touches a curve)

Components: fellow = gent, to beat = tan

TAN/GENT

Quadripartite key to the Guardian's style (4-3) [Auster]

Definition: 'Quadripartite' = FOUR-WAY

Components: key = F (as in music), the *Guardian*'s style =

our way

F/OUR-WAY

Brummie has a – as one might say – short unfinished book: 'Circle of the Romantic English Composer' (4,7) [Brummie]

Definition: 'Romantic English Composer' = IVOR NOVELLO

Components: 'Brummie has a' = I'VE A, which with the homophone indicator ('as one might say') becomes IVOR, 'short unfinished book' = NOVELL(a), circle = O

IVOR (I've a) NOVELL/O

Definition by inference

Here a key part of the clue may not be indicated directly, but what you are required to do can be inferred.

Here are three typical examples:

Blood bath, though horse is protected (7) [Paul]

Definition: 'Blood bath' = CARNAGE

Components: horse = nag, is protected = in care

CAR<NAG>E

Immature tripe ingredient in Bali dish (5) [Rover]

Definition: 'dish' = BALTI (the Indian stew)

Components: immature = not ripe, t(ripe) = T

BAL<T>I

Grudging approval for Rowse? (5,2,5) [Gordius]

Definition: 'Grudging approval' = COULD BE WORSE

Components: Rowse is an anagram of ('could be') = WORSE

You are now armed with the essential tools required to break the codes used by the setters. On looking at a clue, you first have to decide which word (or words) represents the definition of the solution that you are seeking. Then you must read the clue as a whole to decide which of the available cryptic tricks or combination of tricks the setter may have used in writing it.

In the examples used so far in this chapter, almost all the clues have been illustrations of a single type of setting device. Often, though, a setter will mix more than one device in a single clue, each one being identified in that case by a separate indicator word (or words). So, to complete this chapter, here are three groups of ten clues each for you to practise with. They deploy the full range of standard setting conventions.

The clues in Group A come with a note as to which bit of the clue is the definition and an indication as to which setting device(s) is/are involved in the particular clue. In Group B, the clues come just with a note of the device(s), so you will have to work out the definition bit for yourself. In Group C, you are on your own.

In addition, with each clue, some letters of the right answer have already been filled in for you. (This is, in practice, how you would be solving clues, once you had managed to fill one or two correct answers into the grid.) The answers to the clues, plus notes on how they were intended to work, will be found at the end of this chapter.

Practice Clues

Group A

(i) College set on having Sunday off (4) [Rover]

Definition: College

Device(s) used: subtraction

_ _ O _

(ii) Carrying voice of a writer (6) [Audreus]

Definition: writer

Device(s) used: double definition

_ E _ _ _ W

(iii) Novel having pride without prejudice (6,4) [Rufus]

Definition: Novel

Device(s) used: charade

V _ _ _ _ _ F _ _ _

(iv) How to cook duck to be eaten by returning emperor (5) [Shed]

Definition: How to cook

Device(s) used: a split combined with a reversal; 0 = a duck in cricket

R _ _ _ T

(v) Knocked-out World Cup team found in the changing room? (6,6) [Hendra]

Definition: found in the changing room?

Device(s) used: anagram

_ _ L _ _ _ P _ W _ _ _

(vi) What sounds like cane, isn't (4) [Paul]

Definition: isn't (i.e. isn't cane)

Device(s) used: homophone

_ _ E _

(vii) Nurse endlessly transmits to mobile receivers (3,6) [Auster]

Definition: mobile receivers

Device(s) used: subtraction, then charade

C _ _ _ _ D _ O _

(viii) Punishment about a cab I left on which I should be paid (4,3) [Araucaria]

Definition: on which (i.e. a cab) I should be paid

Device(s) used: personification of a tax; charade with a split and a subtraction

R _ _ _   _ _ X

(ix) Municipal convenience switched round to make it PC (5,7) [Gordius]

Definition: PC

Device(s) used: charade reversed

P _ _ _ _   _ _ U _ _ _ L

(x) Tree that old Iberians might have found funny? (7,8) [Janus]

Definition: Tree

Device(s) used: cryptic clue

_ P _ _ _ S _   C _ _ _ _ _ _ _

Group B

(i) Fear arrest (9) [Shed]

Device(s) used: double definition

A _ _ R _ _ _ N _

(ii) All of a tingle from such a beating? (12) [Rufus]

Device(s) used: anagram

F _ _ G _ _ _ _ _ I _ _

(iii) Features mentioned by those who have voted (4,3,4) [Taupi]

Device(s) used: homophones

A _ _ _ A _ _ _ O _ S

(iv) Five hundred like some cakes chopped (5) [Paul]

Device(s) used: charade (Roman numbers are crossword regulars)

D _ C _ _

(v) Intrigue born in Derry manger (11) [Bunthorne]

Device(s) used: anagram

G _ _ _ _ M _ _ D _ _

(vi) The sign changes when you subtract 5 (5) [Quantum]

Device(s) used: subtraction (involving another Roman number)

_ R _ E _

(vii) Bound like the Buena Vista Social Club (8) [Gordius]

Device(s) used: cryptic clue

B _ _ _ A _ E _

(viii) 'Riding is cycling' (Casablanca girl) (6) [Logodaedalus]

Device(s) used: anagram

I _ _ R _ D

(ix) No longer tender, tip of finger when dipped in butter (5) [Brummie]

Device(s) used: single letter (from the end this time) splitting a word (NB a butter can butt)

G _ O _ T

(x) Work nicely with leaders of extreme nationalists to achieve tolerance (8) [Arachne]

Device(s) used: anagram (including two initial letters)

L _ N _ _ _ C _

Group C

(i) The Pony Express's first new recruit (8) [Rufus]

N _ O _ H _ T _

(ii) Criminals stop leaving presents (6) [Bonxie]

O _ F _ R _

(iii) Obedient, but under threat at first in swirling fluid (7) [Moley]

D _ T _ F _ L

(iv) Transport unfortunately isn't arriving (6,6) [Gordius]

V _ R _ I _ T _ A _ N _

(v) Music based on Spooner's bloody muse (5,5) [Araucaria]

M _ O _ Y _ L _ E _

(vi) Time-honoured substitute for 'gaoled' (3-3) [Audreus]

_ G _ - O _ _

(vii) Queen, said to be dead, wrapped in British flag (6) [Logodaedalus]

B _ N _ E _

(viii) Reason traditionally lost at Oxford (5) [Gordius]

_ A _ S _

(ix) Report of wage much below minimum leads to investigation (8) [Araucaria]

S _ R _ T _ N _

(x) Tabloid South American boat handler's reported dispute (4-5) [Brummie]

A _ G _ - _ A _ G _

Solutions to practice clues

Group A

(i) ETON – (s)ET ON [Sunday = S]

(ii) BELLOW – [Saul Bellow]

(iii) VANITY FAIR – [pride = vanity, without prejudice = fair]

(iv) ROAST – TSA<O>R (rev) [emperor = tsar]

(v) TALCUM POWDER – world cup team (anag)

(vi) BEET – beat (homophone)

(vii) CAR RADIOS – CAR(e) RADIOS [nurse = care]

(viii) ROAD TAX – RO<A>D TAX(i) [rod = punishment]

(ix) PRIVY COUNCIL – council privy (rev)

(x) SPANISH CHESTNUT – a tree and an old Spanish (Iberian) joke

Group B

(i) APPREHEND – double def

(ii) FLAGELLATION – all of a tingle (anag)

(iii) AYES AND NOES – eyes and nose (homophones)

(iv) DICED – D/ICED [500 = D]

(v) GERRYMANDER – Derry manger (anag)

(vi) ARIES – (v)ARIES [5 = V]

(vii) BANDAGED – cryptic def [BVSC members are all now older]

(viii) INGRID – riding (anag) [Bergman in *Casablanca*]

(ix) GROAT – G<(finge)R>OAT [English silver coin, not legal tender since the seventeenth century; a goat butts]

(x) LENIENCY – nicely + E,N (anag)

Group C

(i) NEOPHYTE – the pony E (anag)

(ii) OFFERS – OFF(end)ERS [stop = end]

(iii) DUTIFUL – U,T fluid (anag)

(iv) VIRGIN TRAINS – isn't arriving (anag)

(v) MOODY BLUES – bloody muse (Spoonerism and/or anag)

(vi) AGE-OLD – gaoled (anag)

(vii) BANNER – B<ANNE>R ['Queen Anne is dead'; British = BR]

(viii) CAUSE – cryptic def [Oxford is 'the home of lost causes']

(ix) SCRUTINY – SCRU/TINY [screw (homophone) + much below minimum = tiny]

(x) ARGY-BARGY – Argentinean (tabloidese)/bargee (homophone)

Three

Vocabulary, grammar and jargon

The previous chapter, by focusing on the basic devices of the cryptic crossword, may have given the impression that there are clear, universally accepted and enforced rules. The delight of this type of puzzle, however, derives precisely from the fact that this is not the case, that it is a game between individual setters and solvers in which anything goes, provided that all those involved consider it to be fair.

In this, cryptic crosswords have much in common with cricket. Accepted conventions and mannerly conduct are the key to an enjoyable game, rather than binding laws. The conventions involved are arcane, often unintelligible to the newcomer. As with cricket, hours – days even – of endeavour can end without a clear result, but with everyone still having had a good time.

Perhaps this explains why the flowering of the cryptic crossword in the last half-century has been centred in the British Isles and in the other parts of the cricket-playing world – Australia, New Zealand, South Africa, the Indian subcontinent and the Caribbean – although good cryptic crosswords can be found in non-cricket-playing parts of the world.

For example, in the United States they are published by magazines such as *Atlantic Monthly*, the *Nation* and *New York Magazine* (to which Stephen Sondheim contributed diabolically difficult puzzles where his clues fully matched the ingenuity of his lyrics). But, in general, crossword puzzles elsewhere in the world are based on definitional clues, either straight or perhaps involving riddles and ambiguities, or just plain anagrams. For example, a 1997 *New York Times* puzzle with a theme on the world of computers contained clues such as 'Digital monitor' for MANICURIST and 'Hard drive' for TIGER'S TEE SHOT. This class of clue based on a cryptic definition alone appears in our cryptics as well, as a kind of '& lit' clue.

Such puzzles can involve considerable ingenuity on the part of the setters. On the day of the 1996 US Presidential election, the *New York Times* puzzle contained the clue, 'Lead story in tomorrow's newspaper'. It could be completed as either CLINTON ELECTED or BOB DOLE ELECTED, because intersecting clues also had alternative solutions.

(BAT or CAT, for example, were alternative answers to 'Black Halloween animal' to provide the cross-checking B or C as required.) But this kind of puzzle is not a full-blown cryptic as we know it and would not satisfy the demands of *Guardian* solvers.

It follows that, for cryptic crosswords to work, there has to be common ground, shared points of cultural and historical reference, mutually accepted assumptions and prejudices, and a similar sense of humour between setter and solver. In other words, the cryptic crossword is inevitably culture-specific. So the tone and content of a *Guardian* cryptic will differ from, say, a cryptic in the *Daily Telegraph*, the *Daily Mirror*, *The Scotsman*, the *Irish Times*, the *Indian Express* or *Private Eye*, even though in all of these puzzles you will encounter the basic setting devices described in the previous chapter.

This next section will, therefore, set out some of the kinds of vocabulary and styles of language that you will find in *Guardian* cryptics. Many of the same conventions will apply to puzzles published elsewhere, but some will not. It is not in any way an exhaustive list, but is intended as a crash course in the basics of 'crosswordese'.

Abbreviations

As a general rule, abbreviations are only allowed where they are recognised as legitimate by either Collins or Chambers. A short selection of typical abbreviations that you will encounter follows.

'Note' or 'key' in a clue could indicate (musically) A, B, C, D, E, F or G.

B	book, born, bishop, second-class
C	cold, caught, century
D	died
E	English
F	fellow, female, Fahrenheit, loud (musically)
G	gallon, gramme
H	hospital, hot
I	one, the first person
K	kilo, king
L	left, large, lake, Latin, learner, a student
M	metre, male, married
N	name, new, noon
O	nothing, love, duck
P	quiet, soft (musically), page, parking
Q	question, queen
R	right, river, run(s)
S	saint, small, second(s)
T	time
U	universal, university, socially acceptable, posh
V	against, opposed to, very
W	west(ern), wicket, with
X	cross, kiss, vote
Y	yen, yuan
Z	last, zero, zone

Two-, three- and multi-lettered abbreviations are also used. For example:

AA	non-drinkers, drivers
AI (A1)	first-class, (major) road
BA	degree, graduate
BO	a personal problem
CA	(chartered) accountant
CH	child, church, companion (of honour)
DEB	beginner, new girl
EA	each
ENG	England, English

FF	very loud
FBI	(American) cops
GI	private soldier (US)
GP	doctor, group
HE	(His/Her Excellency) for ambassador/governor
HP	(horse) power, sauce
IC	in charge
IOU	debt
JP	magistrate
KG	knight (of the Garter)
KT	knight (plain)
LAB	political party
LSD	(old) money, drug
MA	degree, graduate
MB/MO	doctor/ medical officer
MC/MM	decoration (military)
MS	manuscript, papers, writing
NI	Northern Ireland, province, Ulster
NT	books/(of the) Bible
OB	old boy, outside broadcast
OS	(very) large
PA	father
PB	paperback
PM	afternoon, Tony Blair
QC	silk
QT	(on the) quiet
RA	painter (Royal Academician)
RT	right
RY/RLY	(railway) lines
SH	quiet, silence, mum
SP	odds (starting price)
SS	saints, a ship, (German) secret policemen
TT	race (Isle of Man motorcycles)
TV	the box
UHT	milk
VAT	tax
WI	the Caribbean, women's organisation
XL	extra large
YR	year
ZZ	sleep

Here are three examples of clues involving abbreviations:

To right a wrong (4) [Bonxie]

Definition: 'a wrong' in civil law = TORT

Components: To, right = rt

TO+RT

Brummie's very into artist once worshipped in Rome (7) [Brummie]

Definition: 'once worshipped in Rome' (the Roman goddess of wisdom) = MINERVA

Components: Brummie's = MINE (in a Brummie clue), very = V, artist = RA (member of the Royal Academy)

MINE/R<V>A

Calendar girls' organisation needs externally organising uprightly (7) [Bunthorne]

Definition: 'uprightly' (i.e. standing on end) = ENDWISE

Components: 'Calendar girls' = WI (members of the Women's Institute posed for that calendar), anagram indicator = 'organisation', 'needs' to be placed externally

NEE<WI>DS

Geography and science

There are, of course, many specialised walks of life that also throw up generally recognised abbreviations. N, S, E and W often appear as 'bearings', 'directions', 'points' or 'quarters'. N and S also crop up as '(magnetic) poles', or as 'opposites that attract'. And you will meet all the thirty-two intermediate points of the compass as well, such as NE, NNE, ENE etc. For instance:

Bearing slash from sword (4) [Bunthorne]

Definition: 'sword' = EPEE

Components: bearing = E(ast), slash = pee (as in urinate)

In the crossword world, Devon and Cornwall (plus, at a pinch, Somerset and Dorset) are SW, while Kent is SE and Tyneside NE. In London, the City part is EC and the West End is WC. For instance:

One's home in the Kent area's good for gardening (5) [Quantum]

Definition: 'good for gardening' = SPADE

Components: One's home = PAD, the Kent area = SE

S<PAD>E

Many countries have recognised abbreviations for their full names; AUST, CAN, DEN, FR, GER, IND, KEN, MEX, NOR, NZ, PORT, SA, SP and US(A) are obvious examples. Setters, however, also use the international car registration letter or letters for a country in their solutions. In this system Canada would be CDN, Denmark DK, France F, Germany D, Norway N, Portugal PL, South Africa ZA, Spain E and so on. For instance:

Cadet nearly reaching New Zealand – a solo passage (7)
[Don Putnam]

Definition: 'solo passage' (a virtuoso passage in a piece of music) = CADENZA

Components: Cadet nearly = CADE(t), New Zealand = NZ, a = A

CADE+NZ+A

The American states regularly provide useful initials for setters, who like to confuse you by using the word 'state' in a clue as meaning 'to declare'. All fifty US states turn up from time to time, but the most frequent visitors seem to be California (CAL), Georgia (GA), Massachusetts (MASS), New York (NY), Rhode Island (RI) and Virginia (VA), plus the nation's capital (DC). LA can be either a state or 'American city' (Louisiana or Los Angeles) and so can New York (though, as Americans know, New York City is properly NYC). A recent development to beware of is that setters have started to use the zip code letters for California, which can thus also appear as CA. Incidentally, a list of US state capitals is a handy thing to have. For example, not everyone knows that Bismarck is the capital of North Dakota (ND). Here is such a clue:

Free bear in state not far away (6) [Hazard]

Definition: 'not far away' = NEARBY

Components: anagram indicator = 'free', state = N(ew) Y(ork)

N<EARB(part anagram)>Y

Appearing less frequently are Canadian provinces (Alberta/AB, British Columbia/BC, New Brunswick/NB etc) and Australian states (New South Wales/NSW, South Australia/SA and Northern Territory/NT).

The main contribution that science makes to cryptic crossword clues is via the alphabetical symbols given to chemical elements. There are well over a hundred. The elements with single-letter symbols appear often: carbon (C), fluorine (F), hydrogen (H), iodine (I), nitrogen (N), oxygen (O), phosphorous (P), potassium (K), sulphur (S) and uranium (U). But three two-letter elements – gold (AU), silver (AG) and tin (SN) – appear even more frequently, because they are handy words to work into clues. The handiest of all to the setter is lead (PB), because it is one of those words that can be pronounced in two different ways: as a metal and as a verb meaning to guide. The past tense of the verb, led, is confusingly also a homophone for the metal. You have been warned.

Here is a chemical clue:

Long story about silver found in South Africa (4) [Hazard]

Definition: 'Long story' = SAGA

Components: silver = AG, South Africa = SA

S<AG>A

Fun and games

A knowledge of the terminology of cricket is a fairly essential part of a solver's armoury, but you do not need to know anything about the game itself, its history or how it is played. Interest in cricket is not required, just the terminology. But, if you do not know that a playing session is an innings (singular despite the 's', just like the more logically spelled inning in baseball), that a cricket ground has an infield and an outfield, that an over consists of six balls or deliveries, or that on and off are sides of the field rather than stage directions (and that leg in this context = on), or that run, duck, four, six, wide, bouncer, century, test, Lord's, Oval and Ashes are technical sporting terms, then you will undoubtedly have problems sorting out quite a few clues. For baseball your vocabulary can be more or less limited to home run, first base, pitcher and short stop.

Here are two examples of cricketing clues:

Late cricket session scheduled (7) [Hectence]

Definition: 'Late' = OVERDUE

Components: cricket session = OVER, scheduled = DUE

OVER+DUE

One who doesn't believe near the wicket Derbyshire opener should shift (7) [Paul]

Definition: 'One who doesn't believe' = INFIDEL

Components: near the wicket = INFIELD, Derbyshire opener = D

INFI(D)EL(D) (the 'D' needs to be shifted)

Other games and sporting heroes make quite regular appearances in cryptic clues, but again the knowledge of them required to find the answer is quite superficial. For instance, if you know that there are eleven players in a soccer team and that the FA is the sport's governing body in the UK, and that in rugby union (RU) there are fifteen per side and a try is an achievement rather than merely an attempt, then that is pretty much all that you'll need. The thirteen-a-side version of the game, rugby league, does not seem to feature in crosswords. OG for own goal sometimes appears.

With golf you need to know that pars, birdies, eagles and albatrosses are part of the scoring system, that 'fore' is a warning cry to avoid someone being hit by a stray ball and that the aim is to get to a green and sink a putt. The names of some of the clubs to be found in a golf bag will also come in useful, but you otherwise need not have participated, even to the level of watching the Masters from Atlanta, Ga.

As for the technicalities of other organised games, it will

generally be enough for you to know that bully is a verb at hockey and that the end of this game is full-time; that ice hockey is played with a puck; that in archery the target is made up of concentric circles called bulls, inners and outers, or gold, red, blue and white; that an area for boxing with four corners is, for some reason, called a ring, that a boxing match is a bout and that a KO ends one prematurely; that eights, fours and pairs (as well as being playing cards) are used in competitive rowing; and that in the Olympics, and other games, gold, silver and bronze are first, second and third, respectively. Some setters also show an interest in games such as darts and snooker. But, again, the level of detailed knowledge required to keep up with them is not excessive. In snooker, there are red and coloured balls, with the most valuable being the black, and you pot them or go 'in off' by mistake. With darts, the only out-of-the-way word that it is worth remembering is the name for the brass strip or marker behind which the thrower is required to stand. It is an oche and tends to appear cryptically in clues as some form of 'firing line'.

Sporting personalities are to be found in cryptic clues and their solutions, particularly if they have short names made up of convenient letters, like Ernie Els, the South African golfer. But, dead or alive, they will tend to be sporting figures of sufficient prominence to have made it out of the sports pages and onto the general news or even the front pages of news papers. Among other golfers, Tiger Woods will appear, as well as other all-time greats, such as the Americans Jack Nicklaus and Arnold Palmer. Henry Cotton (1907–87, three times British Open champion) still occasionally crops up.

This illustrates a general point. A cryptic crossword is not specialised. With very few exceptions, the words and names used are those that might be found in a current book or article written for a non-specialised audience. So Babe may lead to Ruth (whose score of 714 home runs hit stood as a record until 1974, though he stopped playing in 1935) or Rocky to Marciano (who became the heavyweight champion of the world in 1952 and retired in 1956, having won every single one of the forty-nine fights in his professional career). And you must expect to rub shoulders with the likes of Ali/Clay, Bannister, Becker, Beckham, Bradman, W.G. Grace, Hutton, Lara, Jesse Owens and Sherpa Tensing.

Among the sedentary games, you need to know that bridge has suits (which can indicate clubs, diamonds, hearts, spades or trumps) and is played by four players (known as north, south, east and west) in two competing pairs, with the partners sitting facing each other. So 'partners' can lead to N with S or E with W and 'opponents' to N or S with E or W. Taking all the tricks is a 'grand slam', which can also come out of a clue about RU or tennis. The pieces and men of the chessboard (e.g. castle/rook/R and pawn/P) often appear and you need at least to know that, in standard chess notation, R = takes (from the Latin word *recipe*, meaning take). You should also remember that a huff is a technical term in the game of draughts.

Here is a sporting clue involving at least a basic knowledge of the Marquis of Queensberry's rules, which regulated boxing from 1869:

Most of my pants are against regulations (5,3,4) [Araucaria]
Double definition
Components: most of my pants are + hitting below the belt is against the Queensberry's rules
BELOW THE BELT

Military matters

Sailors turn up all the time in clues. They can be an AB (Able-bodied Seaman) or an OS (Ordinary Seaman). Individually they can be hand, tar or Jack. Collectively they can be RN (Royal Navy), MN (Merchant Navy) or fleet. Soldiers may appear as GI, OR (other ranks), RA (Royal Artillery/big guns), RE (Royal Engineers), REME (Royal Electrical and Mechanical Engineers) and so on, or just as 'men'. Reservists are often TA (Territorial Army or Terriers). The Royal Air Force shows up less often than the other two services, but you will find the occasional AC or LAC (Aircraftsman/Leading Aircraftsman), and the junior service is particularly useful to setters because of the ambiguity as to whether fliers are the RAF or birds and because a phrase like 'those who fly backwards' produces FAR.

'Officer' and 'decoration' open up the whole range of military ranks and medals (C-IN-C, CO, Colonel, VC, DSO, MC, MM and the rest). Here is a military clue:

Leave soldiers to capture evil thug (7) [Bonxie]
Definition: 'thug' = GORILLA
Components: Leave = GO, soldiers = RA (Royal Artillery), evil = ILL
GO/R<ILL>A

Foreign tongues

Latin still plays a role in cryptic crosswords, at least in its dog Latin form. There are all those words and phrases that have effectively passed into English: *ad libitum* (ad lib, freely), *anno Domini* (AD, in our time, nowadays), *caveat emptor* (let the buyer beware), *circa* (C, CA), *Deo volente* (DV, God willing), *ergo* (so, thus), *exempli gratia* (EG, for example, say), *id est* (IE, that is, that's), *in extremis* (dire straits), *in flagrante* (more dire straits), *nota bene* (NB, note well), *ob/obiit* (he/she has died), *obiter dicta* (a judge's uncalled for remarks), *pro bono publico* (for the public good, unpaid), *quid pro quo* (something for something), *rex/regina* (R), *quod erat demonstrandum* (QED, proof, result), *re* (about, concerning, on), *via* (the Latin way), *quod vide* (QV, reference), *vide* (V, see).

Apart from *hoi polloi*, Greek features hardly at all, except by way of its alphabet (often clued as 'character/letter from Athens/Greece/abroad'). Alpha, beta, gamma, delta and pi are the most familiar, since they are widely used in mathematical and scientific contexts. But the other nineteen letters will turn up as well. Remember that 'the last in Greece' is omega, not zeta.

Here is an example of the sort of clue you will meet:

It's not very long after love letter (7) [Enigmatist]
Definition: 'letter'= OMICRON (the Greek 'O')
Components: It's not very long = MICRON (an invisible fraction of a metre), love = O
O+MICRON

Setters assume that solvers have at least schoolboy/girl French. So LE, LA, LES, DE, DU, DES, A LA, AU, AUX and ET will appear in clues as 'the French', 'French articles' or 'and in France' as appropriate. 'A French' may well lead to UN or UNE. You should also note that, cryptically, 'a Frenchman' can indicate M (monsieur).

The equivalent little words from German (DER, DIE, DAS, EIN, EINE, UND), Spanish (EL, LA, LO, LOS, LAS, UN, UNA, E, Y) and Italian (IL, LA, UN, UNO, UNA, E) also appear frequently. But, for these other languages, in general only those words that have effectively passed into English, like Schadenfreude, prima donna and mañana, are likely to trouble you.

Indian words creep in from time to time, though not as much as they did of old when the connections of so many Brits with the subcontinent were close, mainly as a result of service with the British army in India. The tonga still shows up, though in India today that horse-drawn trap has almost universally given way to the motor-rickshaw. The sari and the dhoti are worn in crosswords and the police hit rioters with their lathis (long and heavy wooden sticks). Indian cuisine is becoming increasingly popular.

Here are two examples of foreign language clues:

Banker with a bank in Paris, right? (5) [Bunthorne]

Definition: 'Banker' = RIVER (a river has banks)

Components: a bank in Paris (i.e. in French) = RIVE, right = R

RIVE+R

Roman marbles missing (3,6,6) [Rufus]

Definition: Latin phrase for 'of unsound mind', or when one has lost one's marbles

NON COMPOS MENTIS

Numbers

These play an important part in cryptic clues. First come the Roman numerals. I, II, III, IV, V, VI, IX, X, XI, XX, L, C, D, M and all points between. Purists say that IC is not the correct Latin for 99, which should be XCIX. No doubt the longer four-letter version is what the Romans themselves actually wrote or carved on their monuments, but the *Everyman Encyclopaedia* records IC as having been used in Holland as early as 1599 and what has been good enough for the Dutch for over four centuries is good enough for a *Guardian* crossword.

Here is a clue involving an abbreviation and a Roman numeral:

It's about a hero getting a record 99 (4) [Logodaedalus]

Definition: 'It's about a hero' = EPIC

Components: a record = EP (extended play), 99 = IC

EP+IC

The fact that 'I' can be represented as the figure '1' or as 'one' or 'a' is very helpful to setters. It allows them to write 'one's' to indicate IS and 'a' to indicate 'I' or 'one' or vice versa. Zero (0) is also versatile, as it can be produced by circle, duck, love, naught, nil, nothing, nought, round, zilch and much more besides. From the world of maths, X and Y often feature as 'unknowns'.

Finally, a number in a clue can, beyond its own meaning, have the quite different function of referring to the answer to another clue in the same puzzle. Thus some wording in a clue like 'Mixed 7' may indicate either that an anagram of SEVEN is involved, or that the anagram required is of the letters in the answer to clue No. 7.

Here is a clue based on the possibilities given to the setter by '1':

A cosmetic joke (3-4) [Enigmatist]

Definition: 'joke' = ONE-LINER

Components: A = 1/ONE, cosmetic = (eye)LINER

ONE+LINER

Punctuation

Clues are punctuated to make the words in them look natural and to mislead you. By and large, therefore, you should read them as if the punctuation were irrelevant. A clue containing the phrase 'Third World' is unlikely to be concerned with economic development; it will probably indicate an R (woRld).

The general point about punctuation is most easily illustrated by these three examples.

Fuzzy, not very fit (4) [Quantum] = AGUE (a fit of shivering)
The comma tries to make you read 'not very fit' together, but the answer lies in 'fuzzy not very'
Fuzzy = vague, very = V
(v)AGUE

Mark turns to Nick; some posh schoolboys know it (4,6) [Logodaedalus] = ETON COLLAR
The capital letters of 'Mark' and 'Nick' are designed to make you think of two boys; but here mark = note, and nick = collar (as in arrest)
Definition: 'some posh schoolboys know it'
Components: NOTE(rev) + COLLAR

I say! (8,7) [Bonxie] = PERSONAL PRONOUN

The clue would just be a definition and in no way cryptic, if it were instead written as: 'I, say', since 'I' is indeed an example of a personal pronoun. The clue, as punctuated, is trying to mislead you into thinking in terms of an exclamation.

There are many pairs of words that, when run together, mean something slightly or very different. Good examples would be indeed/in deed, over coat/overcoat and look out/outlook. In an attempt to mislead you, the setter will use the version that suits the wording of the clue, but does not indicate correctly what you have to do. Thus 'indeed' could indicate that, in the required answer, the letters DEED have to be put around some other word. 'Overcoat' could indicate that you have to reverse the letters COAT to get TAOC; or that some other word has to be put on top of ('over') COAT; or that an anagram ('over') of COAT is required. 'Outlook' could indicate an anagram ('out') of LOOK, or that the letters LOOK have to be put outside some other word. In the same way, 'innate' could indicate that the letters NATE should be placed outside some other word; and the phrase 'uncovered by' could mean that the letters UN are to be covered by some other word.

In this example of such a clue, the first word has to be 'deconstructed' to get the solution:

Inform a friend (9) [Auster] = CLASSMATE

The word 'Inform' has to be read as 'In form'

The apostrophe s is much used by setters, because of its hidden ambiguity. It can be the normal possessive form (of or belonging to), or it can be a contraction of either 'has' or 'is'. When you see a clue with an apostrophe s, always remember that, while in the clue it may seem to be one of the three forms, in cryptic terms it may well be one of the other two. For example, the phrase 'the king's Evil' could lead to the solution via any of the three 'apostrophe' routes: a) the evil associated with the king; b) the king is evil; or c) the king has evil.

When a clue ends with ? or !, it may just be that the surface meaning of the clue requires this punctuation, i.e. that it is in the form of a question, an exclamation or a command. Otherwise, the punctuation may be letting you know that things are not straightforward. For example, there could be a pun involved, or a cryptic definition, or a generic definition.

Here are two examples of clues where the punctuation is telling you that a word is not being used in quite the normal way:

Preliminary excitement at promotion? (10) [Janus]
= PREFERMENT

Definition: 'promotion'

'PRE' is being used out of place as a prefix with the meaning 'before in time', or 'preliminary', excitement = FERMENT

Little known move! (3,2,3,3) [Bonxie] = OUT OF THE WAY

Double definition

'Little known' = out of the way, but 'move' is not (as it might seem) a noun; it is a command to move

Jargon

Any particular group or activity tends to develop its private jargon and crosswords are no exception. But the amount of setters' jargon is not huge and you will pick it up soon enough, particularly if you check the published solutions to clues you cannot solve. However, it has come to be accepted that a few key words have conventional meanings in cryptic crosswords, which are not be discovered in dictionaries or other reference books.

Again, it would be an impossible task to give a complete glossary of such words and phrases, but what follows is intended to give you a flavour of what you will meet in *Guardian* puzzles. It is usually the case that a word or name has become part of crossword jargon and remained current because it is short and contains vowels, which are desperately needed by a setter struggling to fill a grid.

'Actor' (or 'actress') is a good example. The thespians who might be indicated by a clue containing either word are numberless. One who would probably not spring to mind would be Sir Herbert Beerbohm Tree (1853–1917), the actor-manager and half-brother to Max Beerbohm, the caricaturist and author of *Zuleika Dobson*. He is a major figure in the history of the stage, but hardly a household name today. In crossword jargon, though, TREE means actor and vice versa. So, too, do MAE and WEST (1892–1980), though she also features via clues involving life jackets/preservers, because her generous bust made her name the slang term for what allied airmen wore when ditching in the sea in the Second World War. From the ranks of the living, if no longer acting, SHIRLEY and TEMPLE are also conventional partners in clues or solutions.

In the same kind of way, 'port' or 'foreign port' could indicate anywhere in the world, but Aden and Rio are short and have a high vowel count, so appear frequently. 'Old city' has a strong tendency to be Ur, the Babylonian city once on the Euphrates, even though its heyday was the third millennium BC. The royals have developed a jargon, too. In death as in life, Di is a princess; ER, GR, VR stand for monarchs past and present; Cole is an old and/or merry king; Alfred, Catherine and Peter are all great; Ivan is terrible.

With clothing, by far the most common item is the brassiere, which turns up as BRA via endless variations on the theme of 'support' or 'supporter'. 'T' is often there as a kind of shirt, when it is not a kind of junction.

In the real world of politics there is no shortage of dictators, past and present, but Idi Amin, who became unemployed in 1979, and Benito Mussolini, whose career ended even longer ago in 1945, are the crossword's regulars: the first because his name is short and full of vowels, the second because there are lots of words containing the letters DUCE.

Historical figures, particularly Americans, pass through on a regular basis. Lincoln and both Roosevelts translate as ABE, TEDDY and FDR, respectively. He may have been on the losing side in the Civil War, but 'general' very often means LEE. Because he can so conveniently be clued as a direction, Lord NORTH (who lost GR III his US colonies) crops up regularly as PM.

There is also a convention, applying mainly to a handful of dead men of letters, that family names can be translated to initials. Thus Barrie is JM, Milne AA, Lawrence either DH or TE, Shaw GBS, Wells HG and Wodehouse PG. It used in the same way to be quite common for FE to represent that great lawyer-politician, the first Earl of Birkenhead (F.E. Smith), but that convention is definitely on its last legs.

Finally, in the ragbag of crossword jargon appearing in

clues and solutions, Che (Guevara), together with Lenin and sometimes trot means revolutionary; Erica and ling appear more frequently as names for heather than they do in most garden centres; easy = a midshipman (because of Captain Frederick Marryat's 1836 classic, if now little read, novel, *Mr Midshipman Easy*); jolly = a Royal Marine (RM), though it must be some time since this bit of Victorian slang was used outside a crossword; 'on board', implying on board a steamship (SS, though they no longer exist), invites you to put one S at the beginning and the other S at the end of the solution; and see = ELY, because a see is a diocese and there is a Bishop of Ely, which is a nice short word and its letters constitute the ending to countless adverbs. IAN is a Scotsman, when he is not MAC.

To complete this chapter, here are another three groups of ten clues each, which include examples of the further kind of setters' tricks outlined in this chapter. As with those at the end of the previous chapter, the clues in Group A come with a note as to which bit of the clue is the definition and an indication of which setting device(s) is/are involved. In Group B, the clues come just with a note of the device(s). With Group C, you are again on your own. The answers to the clues, plus notes on how they are intended to work, will be found at the end of the chapter.

Practice Clues

Group A

(i) Slow or fast, love? (5) [Shed]

Definition: Slow

Device(s) used: charade and abbreviation

L _ _ T _

(ii) Private papers destroyed (6) [Rufus]

Definition: Private

Device(s) used: anagram

S _ _ _ E _

(iii) Vulgar person (the Parisian) in the lead (4) [Troll]

Definition: Vulgar person

Device(s) used: split word, plus French and abbreviation

P _ _ _

(iv) 'e wasn't ______ when 'e saw the cakes (6) [Araucaria]

Definition: 'e

Device(s) used: solution requires a cockney accent

A _ F _ _ _

(v) A pure northwest Somerset resort (6-5-4) [Hendra]

Definition: & lit

Device(s) used: anagram including abbreviation

W _ _ T _ N - _ _ P _ _ - M _ R _

(vi) Footballer even more excited than usual (8) [Pasquale]

Definition: Footballer

Device(s) used: cryptic definition of 'more excited than usual'

O _ E _ M _ R _

(vii) Secretive about how old one is, unknown to the last (5) [Gordius]

Definition: Secretive

Device(s) used: charade involving abbreviations

C _ G _ _

(viii) Porous rock, pale blue, with iron and a touch of radon (7) [Rover]

Definition: Porous rock

Device(s) used: charade with abbreviations

A _ U _ F _ _

(ix) Virgin takes delivery of foreign magazine (3,6) [Brummie]

Definition: foreign magazine

Device(s) used: charade

_ E _ _ O _ K _ _

(x) Teased with spin, hooked to outfield . . . well held! (4-6) [Quantum]

Definition: well held

Device(s) used: charade with reversal

D _ E _ - S _ A _ _ _

Group B

(i) I say nothing (3) [Enigmatist]

Device(s) used: charade and abbreviations

_ G _

(ii) Smuggle revolutionary into the Hundred Club (9) [Shed]

Device(s) used: split word, misleading capitals

T _ U _ _ H _ _ _

(iii) There's a singular example of these in ancient history (4) [Rufus]

Device(s) used: hidden clue

_ _ _ S

(iv) Disciple keeps St Edward irritated (8) [Logodaedalus]

Device(s) used: split word plus abbreviations

P _ S _ E _ _ _

(v) Stick Bombay ducks (5) [Bunthorne]

Device(s) used: cryptic definition

L _ T _ I

(vi) Perennial time to storm with anger, being incontinent (9) [Brummie]

Device(s) used: split word with misleading punctuation

A _ T _ A _ _ _ A

(vii) Saw dog wearing lead (7) [Chifonie]

Device(s) used: word in an abbreviation

P _ O _ E _ _

(viii) Burden of golfer upset about total (6) [Bonxie]

Device(s) used: reversal and split word

S _ D _ L _

(ix) Cat breaking a jug the artist returned (6) [Moley]

Device(s) used: anagram and reversed abbreviation

J _ _ _ _ R

(x) Ladies with no servants (5) [Arachne]

Device(s) used: charade using abbreviations

W _ M _ _

Group C

(i) Release from service of French mafia (5) [Shed]

_ E _ O _

(ii) Panic caused by a student with weapon (5) [Beale]

_ L _ R _

(iii) Uncommon facial adornment is bound to hurt (8) [Araucaria]

M _ S _ A _ H _

(iv) Tempest shows god in rage (9) [Rover]

_ A _ N _ T _ R _

(v) Did duck or dat? (5) [Rufus]

_ I _ E _

(vi) Final statement from the bar (4,6) [Quantum]

L _ S _   O _ _ _ R _

(vii) Blair's upset about Unionist funeral (6) [Hectence]

B _ R _ A _

(viii) US city an insect invades soon, I suspect (3,7) [Paul]

_ A _ A _ T _ N _ _

(ix) We hear Rushdie and Fitzgerald, perhaps, are cause of ill feeling (10) [Troll]

S _ L _ O _ E _ L _

(x) Declining years not without love (8) [Beale]

D _ C _ D _ N _

Solutions to practice clues

Group A

(i) LENTO – LENT/O [slow in music; Lent = a time of fast; love = O]

(ii) SAPPER – papers (anag) [Private in the Royal Engineers]

(iii) PLEB – P<LE>B [PB = lead]

(iv) ALFRED – 'e wasn't 'ALF RED when [King Alfred wasn't half red when he saw that he had burned the cakes]

(v) WESTON-SUPER-MARE – a pure NW Somerset (anag)

(vi) OVERMARS – more than just 'over the moon' [Marc

Overmars, formerly of Arsenal and Holland]

(vii) CAGEY – C/AGE/Y [about C; 'how old one is' = age; 'unknown' = Y]

(viii) AQUAFER – AQUA/FE/R(adon)

(ix) NEW YORKER – virgin = new, yorker = cricket ball

(x) DEEP-SEATED – outfield = deep + teased (anag)

Group B

(i) EGO – EG(say)/O

(ii) TRUNCHEON – T<RUN/CHE>ON [smuggle = run (as in gunrunning); revolutionary = Che; hundred = ton]

(iii) THIS – ancienT HIStory [singular of 'these']

(iv) PESTERED – PE<S>TER/ED [disciple = Peter; saint = S; Edward = Ed]

(v) LATHI – cryptic definition

(vi) ASTRANTIA – AS<T/RANT>IA (a hardy perennial) [time = T; storm wth anger = rant; continent = Asia]

(vii) PROVERB – P<ROVER>B [a saw = a saying; dog= Rover; lead = PB]

(viii) SADDLE – E<ADD>LS(part rev) [golfer = (Ernie) Els; total = add]

(ix) JAGUAR – a jug (anag) + RA (rev)

(x) WOMEN – W/0/MEN [with = W; no = O; servants = men]

Group C

(i) DEMOB – DE/MOB

(ii) ALARM – A/L(student)/ARM

(iii) MUSTACHE – MUST/ACHE – 'uncommon' here indicates an alternative spelling of 'moustache'

(iv) RAINSTORM – RA(Egyptian sun god)/IN/STORM

(v) EIDER – a kind of duck and 'either', said with childish lisp, in response to the question 'or that/dat?'

(vi) LAST ORDERS – cryptic def

(vii) BURIAL – B<U>LAIR(part anag)

(viii) SAN ANTONIO – S<AN ANT>OONI(part anag) [an insect = an ant; soon I (anag)]

(ix) SALMONELLA – Salman (Rushdie)/Ella (Fitzgerald) (homophone)

(x) DECADENT – DECADE/N(o)T

Four

Hints and wrinkles

A neurologist might well have interesting things to say about how to tackle crossword puzzles. The way in which each individual's brain records words visually and sorts the letters that form them, and the way in which it tackles questions (and riddles in particular), clearly have a decisive effect on solving clues. All that I am able to offer, however, is empirical evidence of ways of doing crosswords that seem to help many people.

The key point is that a clue is infinitely easier to solve if you have one or more cross-checking letters already filled into the grid. Related to this is the fact that, once you have read a clue and thought about it for a few minutes without being able to solve it, you tend to get stuck in a kind of mental cul de sac.

So, the first thing to do is to skim the clues to see whether a solution leaps out at you. You can either skim all the clues in one go and then settle down to look at the others for which you now have some cross-checked letters; or, having got the answer to one clue, you can set to work to see if you can build a cluster of answers around it. Also, if you become completely stuck on a clue, forget it; make a cup of coffee or leave it until the evening. As often as not, having shut down and rebooted itself, your mind will instantly see the answer that was blocked before.

If you think that you have an answer that may be right, but you are not absolutely sure, do not write it firmly into the grid. Once your brain has visually registered a word, for some reason it finds it extremely difficult to think differently. In particular, the wrong letters inked into the grid will make it much harder to work on any intersecting clues. It is best, in this situation, to record the letters that might contribute to clues in the other direction faintly in pencil. You will find that your mind will then be much more willing to adjust if your initial guess turns out to be wrong.

It also seems that the mind has much more difficulty reading a word that is written vertically than one that is written horizontally. If, therefore, you have some letters in the grid for a Down clue, jot them horizontally in the margin or on another bit of paper. Most people find it hard to see that

_

R

_

_

E

_

T

_

A

might lead to ORCHESTRA, but much easier to see that _ R _ _ E _ T _ A is heading in that direction.

A related trick of the eye concerns anagrams. With the clue 'Orchestra when playing is able to carry a heavy load (9)', it may at once occur to you that an anagram of orchestra could be involved, particularly since the word has nine letters. The answer, though, may not come to you just by staring at 'orchestra'. It is much more likely to jump out at you, if you write the letters down in a jumble. The mind then seems to be freed from the prejudice that those nine letters spell orchestra. In particular, many people find it helpful to write out the letters that are candidates for an anagram in a circle backwards with one letter in the middle:

O

R R

C A T

H S

E

The mind's eye is now much more ready to see that these letters can also spell CARTHORSE.

Setters go to great pains to ensure that the apparent, or 'surface', meaning of their clues is conveyed in words that flow as smoothly – and thus as misleadingly – as possible. But, however much they try, they are not always 100 per cent successful and one word can stick out as not being quite natural to that sentence. Latch onto it at once. It is almost certain to be the key to the clue, either as an indicator of one kind or another, or as (part of) an anagram, or as a cryptic element in a solution.

You will quickly come to recognise the 'sore thumb' in a clue when you see it. For example, if you came upon a clue such as 'Dine less to produce indolence (8)', you would rightly conclude that it lacks any even halfway smooth surface meaning to mislead you. 'To produce' is a pretty obvious anagram indicator (see page 40). The solution requires an eight-letter word and DINE + LESS happen to add up to eight letters. You would rapidly conclude that this is just a bad clue for IDLENESS (indolence).

It is also helpful to remember that there are many common letter combinations and word endings. Most obviously, Q almost invariably goes before U. So, if you already have either a Q or a U in the grid as a contribution to an unsolved clue, try the other with it in your mind to see if that produces some productive idea. C or G with H, and P and T with R are similar examples.

There are some particularly common word endings such as -ABLE, -AL, -ALLY, -ED, -ER, -ELY, -IAN, -IBLE, -ING, -IOUS, -MENT, -TER, -TION and -TOR, which crop up again and again. If you have one of these letters already in the grid towards the end of a solution, try the whole of one or other of these common endings in your mind to see if something clicks.

This advice does not apply only to the clue that you are actually working on. One or other of these possible word endings will also give you potential cross-checking letters for clues in the other direction. Pencil the relevant ones in lightly and test to see whether they may give you a lead there as well.

In the same way, a clue, even if you cannot solve it at once, may make it close to certain that the answer is either a plural word ending in s (though, of course, this is not true of all plurals), or a verb that has to end in s. In this case, you can pencil in an S to see if that gives you any help with a clue in the other direction. A variation on this theme is that, if you have, say, the second letter of a solution already in the grid, you can run through the alphabet in your mind to see if, in combination with the letter already there, any two first letters suggest the right answer.

If there is a linking theme to the hints in this chapter it is this: beginners assume that cryptic puzzles are solved by reading the clues and working out the answers; in reality, you often work from the other end, taking whatever you have already entered in the grid and trying various combinations of letters until you find an answer that makes sense of the clue. You will know that it is the right answer, when you can see how the cryptic part of the clue works to get you there.

Finally, here are some tips for dealing with a kind of clue that is a hallmark of one or two *Guardian* setters: the really long anagram. These can be twenty or more words long and occupy the numbered slots in the grid for several solutions consecutively. Some solvers hate this type of clue and all beginners despair of ever being able to cope with them. You will soon recognise such a clue by the style. There is no chance at all of being able to solve it cold. You first need the help of as many cross-checking letters as possible from other answers. So leave even attempting to solve this particular clue until you have made as much progress as possible with the 'normal' answers.

Then, on a piece of paper, jot down a record of how far you have reached. With luck, this exercise might leave you with something like:

_H_ B__ _T_O_ O_ T__ _U__I_G _E_K

Armed with this data, you could take the next step of identifying which word in the clue is the probable anagram indicator and which words (to include H, B, T, O, O, T, U, I, G, E and K), the anagram fodder.

On top of that, one or both of the two three-letter words _H_ and T__ are likely to be THE, and O_ can really only be OF, ON or OR. By a process of elimination, you should by this stage begin to have an idea of the letters still free to put into the anagram. The final element, though, is that a long anagram clue of this kind will have within itself a hidden or cryptic indication of what the final answer is to be. In this case a good and fair clue should have put the notion of a patriotic or Victorian poem into your mind, helping you to get to:

THE BOY STOOD ON THE BURNING DECK

Explained in theory like this, such a clue will still remain a daunting proposition to a beginner. But cracking a good clue of this sort can yield such a level of satisfaction that it is worth persevering. Here are two classic examples:

Here 'n' there in the heavens' watery mire are tiny slits, so the harsh weather is slight, not bulky, perhaps? (Spike Milligan) (5,3,5,2,3,3,5,3,4,4,2,3,6,4,2,5,5,3,4,2,4) [Paul]

The anagram indicator is 'perhaps?'. The anagram is made up of all that stands before the indicator. And the solution is a nonsense rhyme by Spike Milligan:

THERE ARE HOLES IN THE SKY
WHERE THE RAIN GETS IN,
BUT THEY'RE EVER SO SMALL,
THAT'S WHY RAIN IS THIN

Poetic scene with surprisingly chaste Lord Archer vegetating (3,3,8,12) [Araucaria]

The anagram is of 'chaste Lord Archer vegetating', with 'surprisingly' doing duty here as the anagram indicator. The poem involved in the solution is the one by Rupert Brooke with the church clock standing at ten to three and honey still for tea. The house is now the home of Jeffrey Archer and his wife Mary. The solution is:

THE OLD VICARAGE, GRANTCHESTER

New technology

It is no secret that crossword setters today make extensive use of computer programs. These programs are essentially an outgrowth of computer spellcheckers and the huge stored word lists on which they are based. Their greatest help to setters is in being able to throw up all the available words or phrases of a given length and with specified letters in specific places.

This is a great time-saver. In fact, most such programs can now use their latent capacity to fill an entire grid automatically, or to complete a grid that is already part-filled. They can also offer solutions with a running theme: birds, flowers, Crusader castles. Cryptic clues, of course, still have to be written for the solutions. Here the programs can also help the setter by offering up the full range of anagrams available from any given jumble of letters, or by finding words containing a particular sequence of letters.

This book is written for would-be solvers, not for would-be setters. However, programs designed for setters can be used in reverse by solvers. If you suspect an anagram is lurking in a clue, you can type in the likely word(s) involved and see what other word combinations get thrown up on the screen. If you already have, say, B _ R _ _ _ _ L, your program will probably tell you that only three words or phrases fit: BARONIAL, BAR STOOL and BIRD CALL. Suddenly, the clue that has been baffling you will, no doubt, be obvious. The limitation of these programs is, of course, that they can only work with the words that have been stored in their memories. They will not help you with unusual words or the names of people and places.

Setters, of course, should use the programs. Compiling a good crossword is a laborious business and poorly paid. So any short cut that allows setters to spend more time on writing good clues and less on struggling to find words to fit the grid is a good thing. But *solving* crosswords is supposed to be a recreational activity, providing some mental challenge and a sense of achievement. Using a computer program to find a missing answer seems a bit like cheating at patience or going for a walk and taking a taxi home.

Purists may say that the true path is to solve crosswords without electronic aids, rather like climbing Everest without oxygen. But, for most younger solvers, Googling is a part of life. And for most non-Brits and expats who do British cryptics, Google is a convenient way to get into the culture-specific references that underlie so many cryptic clues. Even so, beware: one solver, who typed a few key words into Google in the hope of finding help with a clue involving sea dogs and pirates, was shunted to a hard-core porn site.

On the other hand, all solvers from time to time use dictionaries and other reference works to check spellings and facts, or to discover things they did not know or to rediscover things forgotten. Such discovery is very much a part of the pleasure of the game. So what, you might say, is the difference between using a dictionary and using a computer program to find a spelling, or between using an encyclopaedia and using Google to find a fact?

The market leader in the UK is undoubtedly Antony Lewis's *Crossword Compiler*. He started the project in order to teach himself computer programming in 1993, when he was doing his A-levels. He is currently a research fellow in cosmology at the University of Toronto, but will be returning to Cambridge by the end of 2005. He sold the first DOS version of his program in 1994. The first Windows version appeared in 1995 and there have been major upgrades every few years ever since. Today the basic package fills grids, finds words and works out anagrams or partial anagrams. His WordWeb Pro add-on is a thesaurus that can find synonyms and related words and definitions and can work from lists of obscure words and phrases, or specialised subjects, geographical names and the like. A high proportion of regular UK compilers use his programs. The website is www.crossword-compiler.com.

Derek Harrison's *The Crossword Centre* at www.crossword.co.uk has a great deal of helpful material. In particular, from his website you can download for free Henry Casson's *Crossword Utility*, which allows you to produce puzzles in one or other of the formats that publishers demand. Another useful tool for finding words with difficult letter combinations and for solving/setting anagrams can also be found at www.wordfun.ca in Peter Bevin's *Crossword Solver*. This uses as its wordbase a list called TEA, compiled originally by Ross Beresford and now to be found at www.bryson.ltd.uk/wordlist.html. The same site also offers SYMPATHY, another program for compiling and submitting puzzles to publishers. Similar software is available in other countries. For example, in Australia, Doug Butler at Flinders University in South Australia has developed a program called 'AxWord for Windows'. His e-mail address is doug.butler@flinders.edu.au.

Dictionaries and reference works are now, of course, available online and in CD-rom or DVD versions, some free, most not. WordWeb has a free thesaurus and dictionary at http://wordweb.info/free/ and a cut-down version at www.wordwebonline.com. The *Encyclopedia Britannica* is online at www.britannica.com and also has a DVD version for sale. xref provides a substantial library of the world's leading reference books at www.xref.com. There is a 6,000 digital page *Crossworder's Dictionary and Gazetteer* at www.crosswordstar.com. Finally, most dictionary publishers also now produce CD or DVD versions of their main works.

Five

Practice puzzles, notes and solutions

This final chapter gives you fourteen cryptic puzzles to play with. They have all been published either in the *Guardian* or on the paper's website, www.guardian.co.uk, where there is an online crossword subscription service.

To give you a helping hand, some of the letters have already been filled into the grids. These, in particular, should get you thinking about possible combinations of letters as word endings. The completed solution grids, with explanations, conclude the chapter.

Puzzle 1

Rufus

Across

1 Some delay in imposing sentence on convict (4-3)
5 Coax little Josephine into ruffled lace (6)
9 Solid grasp of company case? (4,4)
10 Threaten one politician with death (6)
12 The confidence of one taking part (5,7)
15 Musical group stepping out together (6,4)
17 There'll be talk if this is broken (3)
19 Initially thought to come from outer space (3)
20 Unfair bit of gossip? (4,6)
22 Chap involved with literacy in classical form (12)
26 I am given a role to communicate (6)
27 One may be struck for showing off (8)
28 Bearing blossom in March or April (6)
29 Woodpecker knew cry called for change (7)

Down

1 Swell to fortissimo (4)
2 Identify the victim (4)
3 Has a cigarette and looks happier (6,2)
4 Preceding to enter by gate at the front (5)
6 Under treatment, impart personal depression (6)
7 Penitentiary with unlimited accommodation? (4,6)
8 One of the fruits of advanced age? (10)
11 Not a musical score (6)
13 The case for the prosecution? (10)
14 All-star casts? (10)
16 Cricket side gets lucky cup draw with an extra (3,3)
18 The kindness of people (8)
21 The extent to which undergrads work? (6)
23 Two in difficulties, being pulled along (2,3)
24 Solid figure that may take root (4)
25 Growth seen on upturned ship's bottom (4)

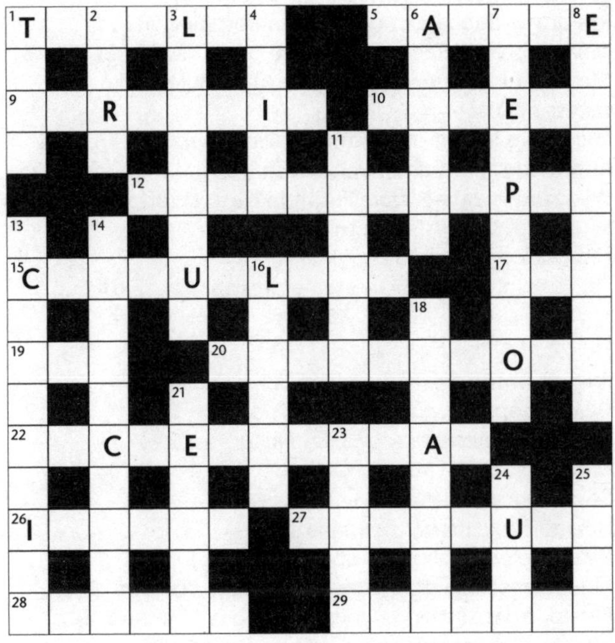

Puzzle 2

Logodaedalus

Across

1 Destroy poster etc, which must be suppressed (3,6)
6 Crawl, perhaps, inside nuns' wimples (4)
10 Terrace where a senior citizen keeps that thing turning (5)
11 Being a cleaner, lift or lie around (3,6)
12 One left leg half rose in a lively manner (7)
13 Resides with Spanish girl, accommodating her (7)
14 Make more efficient as I lock the pin for a change (4,4,5)
17 More than a hairdo and a knees-up would be an excess (13)
21 They have little money for drunken toper? Oh! (3,4)
22 Informed sailor takes river, which leads to the Orient (7)
24 Wicked dog owner gains right to be a lawbreaker (9)
25 Scrap that sounds like a truce (5)
26 Attitude? It's time to acquire one (4)
27 The British duck notices area of fresh water (3,6)

Down

1 Pa gets bottle cracked – it's for VIPs (3,5)
2 Dead poppy head comes up as part of a flower (5)
3 Philosophy of rationing? That will do! (6,2,6)
4 Eliminate source abroad (4,3)
5 Counts everyone seen in neckwear (7)
7 New rafter constructed in plant (5,4)
8 Ill-tempered doctor got up from bed (6)
9 Make printer do graph, which is above criticism (5,3,6)
15 Big editor absorbed in comic, which is to fold (5,4)
16 Idolaters he meets somewhere in Greece (8)
18 Draught wine could be terminal (7)
19 In difficulties, but not grounded? (2,1,4)
20 Shut up for a second, that is to say (4,2)
23 Expert artist seen climbing palm tree (5)

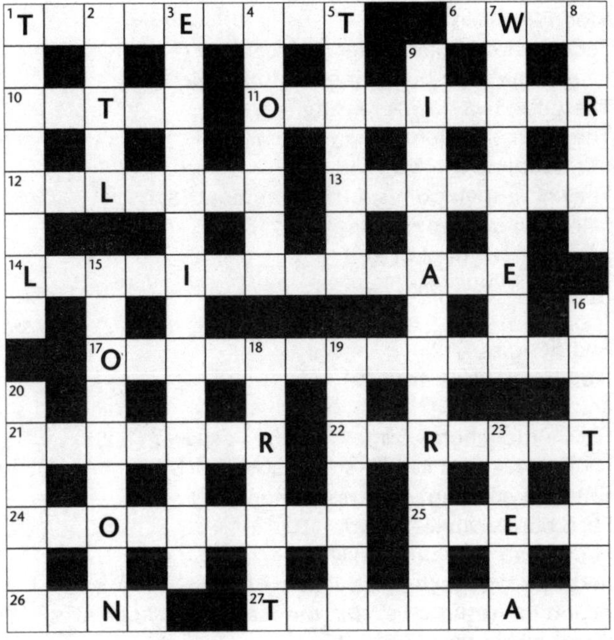

Puzzle 3

Rover

Across

1 This major passed away (6)
5 The Navy's underclass? (8)
9 Crafty creature has cover in plant (8)
10 Sores start suppurating after cruel operation (6)
11 Undemocratic Italian dabbling with tarot (12)
13 Wood for sale (4)
14 People with 'A' start to learn Greek, say (8)
17 River argument shows singer raising voice (8)
18 These fish feel slippery inside (4)
20 They direct random prison search (12)
23 She's rattling the Bar (6)
24 They have their points, but not at night (8)
25 Salesman gets up repeat figures (8)
26 A gift of storybooks (6)

Down

2 Bed design (4)
3 Number on Ali's drug (9)
4 Soft iron (6)
5 How a lucky florist comes out after a shave? (8,2,5)
6 Flighty creatures can be subtle about it (8)
7 Bishop is stabling a champion horse (5)
8 Such books cannot be got (10)
12 Sportsman swinging the lead etc (10)
15 Result of too much oil on lighter? (9)
16 Acting managers and what they say to leaky defences? (8)
19 It flies about throne (6)
21 Bury Football Club (5)
22 Invent aircraft without tailpiece (4)

Puzzle 4

Pasquale

Across

1 Ground or pasture for old beast (9)
6 Strength in something the widow had said (5)
9 Ugly, Iraq? No fun, I'd fancy, in the heat (10,5)
10 Girl in passageway stopping short, looking back (4)
11 Time you recalled workers – end of holiday (3,5)
14 A new fellow can start to operate quite slowly (9)
15 Solid piece about to be taken out of tree (5)
16 Mount with medium-hard mineral at its core (5)
18 I think one should get firm with troublemaker losing head (9)
20 Outlaw making likely end – bad one being suspended (3,5)
21 Blemish is almost frightening (4)
25 Illegal entrant, I exploded something said to be dangerous (1,6,8)
26 One of those letters from abroad soldiers sent back to mum (5)
27 Parliamentarian dog spoke aloud in the style of Spooner (9)

Down

1 Needle in stiff fabric (5)
2 Authorised report of lady's exsanguination (7)
3,17 Singer – man providing lift with revolutionary sound (4,7)
4 Some revolutionary lefties in compound (4)
5 Make an effective stab at providing a short survey (3-7)
6 Steel component in designated habitat for semi-arboreal mammal? (10)
7 Nasty stuff affecting kids could lead to a listener's complaint (4,3)
8 Toy given twist beginning to break, split on the outside (5,4)
12 Not here – but in Rome? (2,8)
13 A taxing time, particularly for Americans (6,4)
14 Olympic entertainers running in heats, carrying a number (9)
17 See 3
19 Touching performance in Derby, say (7)
22 Poor paper – person in charge of it was furious (5)
23 What Cupid bears audibly for lover (4)
24 Bloke getting sacked losing ego (4)

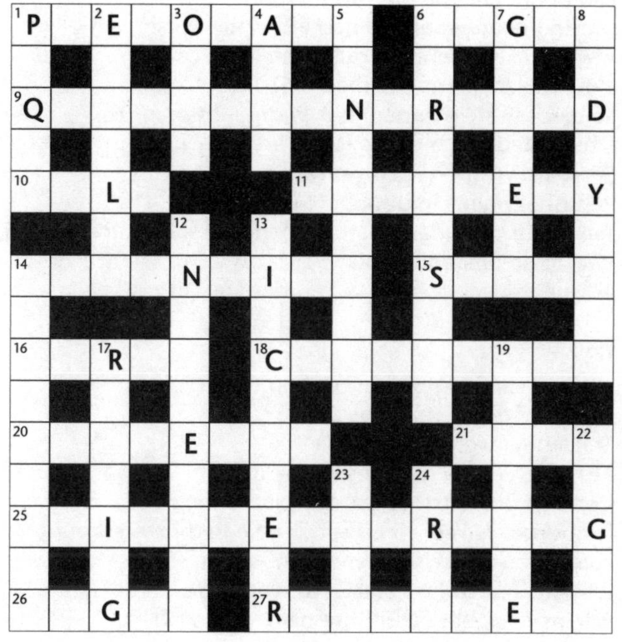

1 P
2 E
3 O
4 A
5
6
7 G
8
9 Q
N
R
D
10
L
11
E
Y
12
13
14
N
I
15 S
16
17 R
18 C
19
20
E
21
22
23
24
25
I
E
R
G
26
G
27 R
E

Puzzle 5

Janus

Across

1 Powerful figure in grip of drug (6)
4 Jesting at one attempting to slim (6)
9 Surface with Scotch tar mixture to meet a requirement (4,2,2,7)
10 Did poor mad Poe put this on top? (6)
11 Moving point wounded nag internally (8)
12 Always taking right girl out, even in defeat (8)
14 Slip away to see pal, perhaps (6)
15 Soldier's vehicle turned over to draughtsman (6)
18 Obliterated when we do it up carelessly (5,3)
21 Standard weapon in conversation (8)
22 Publishes points in dispute (6)
24 Talks with couturier before audience at stately home (10,5)
25 Way to go on gentle walk (6)
26 Advantageous to America to order fuel (6)

Down

1 Suggest showing professional attitude (7)
2 Centre of nest remains as orifice (5)
3 Small boys with pincers? (7)
5 Attribute certain qualities to a writer (7)
6 Conduct orchestral rehearsals for the militia (9)
7 Renounces former creed and is able to throw rest out (7)
8 Force the Spanish to follow competition (6)
13 It uplifts one to find oracles at work (9)
16 Attains goal, but feels those pains again (7)
17 Frenchman brought up law's restoration (7)
18 Turned aside to take in female by boat (6)
19 Becomes engaged in predicaments (7)
20 Note unusual lines of vessel (7)
23 Express derision at meal (5)

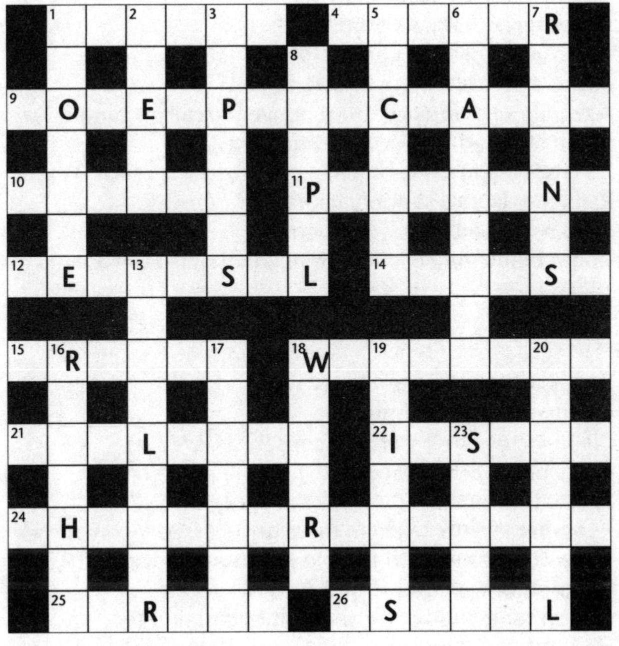

Puzzle 6

Arachne

Across

1 Man following rough bunch of soldiers (7,5)
8 Propensity to be not entirely straight (7)
9 Bats native to a bit of marsh in southeast Asian country (7)
11 To misrepresent late Princess is wrong (7)
12 Colonist translated letters (7)
13 Relish being in Rita's tent! (5)
14 I bet Arnie collapsed drunk (9)
16 I sang a lot about homesickness (9)
19 A couple of guards confront convict in prison camp (5)
21 Bread is mixed, then cooked slowly (7)
23 US city's noisy gangs initially disturbed our relaxed mood (7)
24 Refined chap's a slippery character! (7)
25 Press some levers to work loom (7)
26 Could be extremely effective new Rangers FC manager (6,6)

Down

1 Paddy Reed is an informer (7)
2 Offensive rumour about title (7)
3 Claim victory over German conservatives (5,4)
4 Has a home over in Seville (5)
5 Article on Her Majesty's, say, for Americans (7)
6 Reprobate finally taken in by reformed fallen woman (7)
7 Piece of luggage with flexible bands and a toggle (9,3)
10 Sell plot for fruit and veg (6,6)
15 Girl's after last bit of brocade for decoration (9)
17 He carefully examines girl in Senior Common Room (7)
18 Serious European support for American writer (7)
19 Sing about English plant (7)
20 Left a subordinate to wash clothes (7)
22 Leading detective starts to examine leads and vital evidence in search for information (5)

Puzzle 7

Araucaria

Across

1 Among French articles supporting present to sailor it's beyond absolution (13)
10 On one hitting that way, I should be busy on April 1st (3-6)
11 Classical beauty spot invokes cutting mood (5)
12 An ear for future agenda? (5)
13 Look at the first person in surprise (3-6)
14 Imperfectly speaking, exhibit by the Royal Academy ... (7)
16 ... which could be a help to one recently exhibited in the 15 square 4 (7)
18 Draw an abstainer to right performance (7)
20 Source of good food at good height gives pleasure (7)
21 Over half a mile round is south Indian city's affectionate greeting (9)
23 Group unable to work online? (5)
24 Strap may follow report of some difference (5)
25 Grandee's witchcraft includes backing female in love (9)
26 16's fellows pause for thought before man with a life goes to fish (7,6)

Down

2 Shady glen with one fellow not taking care (9)
3 Handy to get oxygen to melt (2,3)
4 Take in cookhouse on the top floor (7)
5 A lot of worms pause for thought, being previously exhibited in the 15 square 4 (7)
6 An inclination a friend has to be Protestant? (9)
7 The world of French, not of fruit (5)
8) (5,8)
9 Filling place for head removed from hospital, rotten, to be reformed (6,7)
15 Battle time for service on much of Portuguese coast (9)
17 National rating, one other (9)
19 Cooking – try mash – current in Anglo-Saxon times (7)
20 Mother's getting on with award of court (7)
22 Row caused by scientist or mathematician (5)
23 Half the folk next door sound like horses (5)

Puzzle 8

Quantum

Across

5 Lady in centre of lake in waterproof clothing (6)
6 City, very large, giving a sense of anticlimax (6)
9 Theatrical American university buildings (6)
10 Army unit to cover half a mile making a call (8)
11 River I shall cut short to get a small one (4)
12 Study effect of power when not in the Union (10)
13 Argue with solver initially taken in by puzzles? (5,6)
18 One writing publicity stuff to indulge in plagiarism? (10)
21 Northern town's lighter part (4)
22 Winning oar blade at sea (8)
23 Aussie pal's personal stuff left out (6)
24 Name target mainly set in place for hitchers (6)
25 New year pupils in remove (6)

Down

1 Come April, losing head could be a trickster (8)
2 Wine – and where you might get it on account (6)
3 'Night' steward (8)
4 The songbird diverted hikers (6)
5 What'll we hear? (6)
7 Do up at Stationery Office is a source of pleasure (6)
8 1 supporting style is one to show the way (11)
14 Girl musicians providing dance music (8)
15 Relaxed movement presented by the conductor (8)
16 Fast food's trouble, tho' cooked first (6)
17 Agree to remove top player, reportedly (6)
19 Delivery man turning up at roadside endlessly (6)
20 Split involving Church not long ago (6)

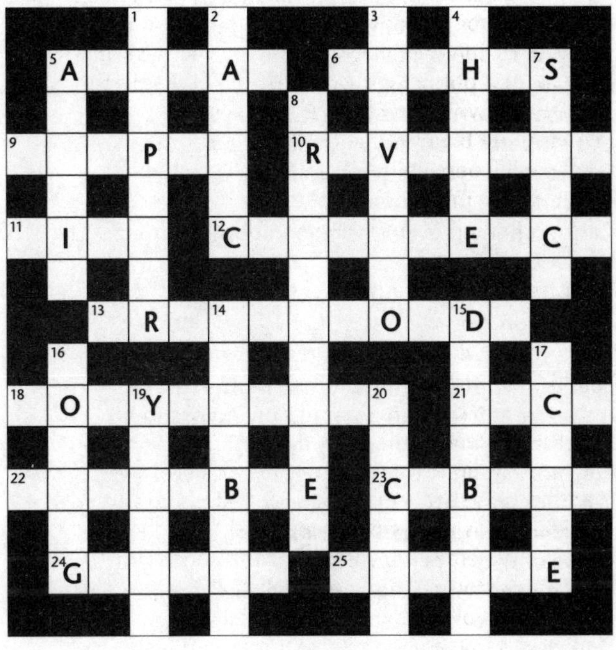

Puzzle 9

Gordius

Across

1 The only good woman abroad – but she's a dish (4,5,5)
9 A girl has to get her weight right for a job at the Beeb (9)
10 Actress with nothing to boast about? (5)
11 Poor student transported on the lower deck (5)
12 Scheme of lover somewhat rudely set aside (9)
13 Uncharacteristic feature of log? (8)
14 Location of Seoul once select (6)
17 24 state of untidy chaos (6)
19 Like many clues in the French game (8)
22 Old emperor is buried in Romberg (9)
24 Public backing to protect a minister (5)
25 Opening of space attempt (5)
26 Cancel opening event for being about a minute overdue (9)
27 6 felt heart beat for a predecessor (6,3,5)

Down

1 Politician with something of the night? (6,8)
2 It's nothing to put on a pound, giving rise to fat (7)
3 Plan for a pornographic picture? (9)
4 Postmortem on rise of currency over harvest (8)
5 What an apprentice may become, but not at first (6)
6 Old king failing to make the grade (5)
7 Game of wits (7)
8 How a handsome curate may look for interest (4,10)
15 Schooling that's acutely distressing? (9)
16 Golf club refreshment (8)
18 Modern technology's at one's fingertips (7)
20 Leak this with a number for cross-reference (7)
21 Honest journalist produced pulp (6)
23 Leo, the first sign given by a philosopher (5)

Puzzle 10

Bonxie

Across

9 Brother found by daycare centre (5)
10 Half-hearted chap ate it, perhaps (9)
11 Fatigue shown by public protecting old monarch (9)
12 He appears among the panellists (5)
13 Strong coffee reaches new level (7)
15 See 3
17,18 Dumb insolence may lead to this (5,3)
20 King stands to the right of drawing board (5)
22 Less blue or more pink (when tickled) (7)
25 Pucker up quietly – flower changes hands finally (7)
26 Singular warlord points to part of bow (5)
27 Case of paper showing concern about finger (9)
30 A cheeky display before Polish liquor (9)
31 It reverses the charge (5)

Down

1 When Barnet is bushy for a change? (4)
2 Men of letters turned on irate doctor (8)
3,15 Brothers order: 'Frank and Mary – embrace child!' (11)
4 Couple with serviceman by the side of the dam (8)
5 Woollen hat found lying under stopcock (6)
6 First, second and third of four by rank, colloquially (5,5)
7 Hot scarf seen on 1 November (6)
8 Book review said to contain them (4)
13 Get chef drunk in time (5)
14 Stew tea: it's a key way to relax (4,2,4)
16 Connect student to peasant (5)
19 Finished with heartless acts? Make cakes! (8)
21 Defending champion? (8)
23 Confer by river – there's nothing in the net (6)
24 Kick about the ring (6)
26 Carry sleeping policeman, maybe (4)
28 Promise of love at hotel (4)
29 Stable fails to complete the race (4)

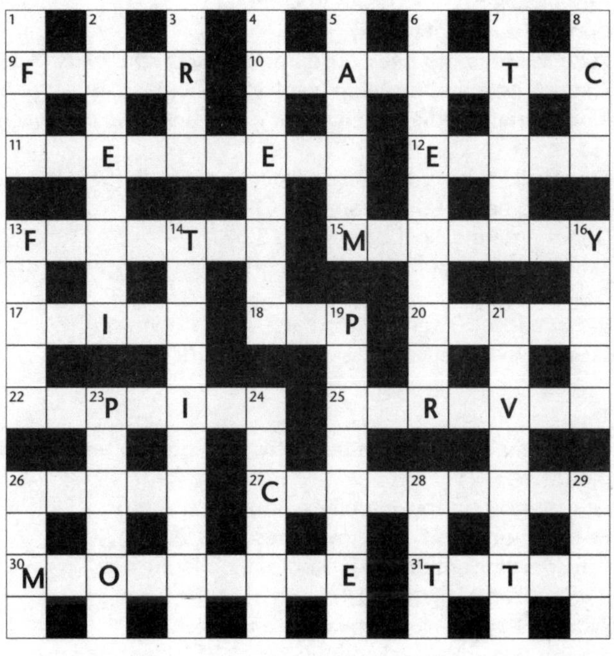

Puzzle 11

Shed

Across

1 Crush a dignitary (5)
4 Mowlam on horseback – turncoat and rabble-rouser (8)
8 How plants grow flowers? Keeping warm, new doctoral research reveals (14)
10 Fabric layer in poor health in church (8)
11 Coming out elliptical (6)
12 Keep maintaining peak condition and seize the reins (4,5)
15 Singer's personal problem involving fool (5)
17 Remuneration Poles received for being anything but macho (5)
18 Terrorists I subsequently sent back come back (9)
19 Very bad habit, taking tabloid (6)
21 Drier item for sale aboard train (3,5)
24 Sanctimonious author in Hamburg's top hotel gets thrown out (6-4-4)
25 It's true love! Given the stomach, I'll do anything! (8)
26 Take to Sky, receiving line from the Sun? (5)

Down

1 Overworks animals – tame one burrowing into the Spanish mountain (12)
2 Smutty stuff on royal family's fabulous afterbirth (9)
3 Ex-boxer catches Zeus's lover dressing (5)
4 Transport for emigrants is a potential bloomer (9)
5 Rugby team's memory (4)
6 Woman torn apart by aristocrat's disaster (9)
7 A truth universally acknowledged at 10.10 in the morning (5)
9 Philosopher – to wit, Hungary's first player taking gold after end of match (12)
13 A scientific figure – pity his science is flawed (9)
14 May her swine's flesh putrefy in Yorkshire! (9)
16 Cricket ground's turned small boy into fan of central Europe (9)
20 Eros reflected on a smell (5)
22 Dog food containers I opened (5)
23 Summons jester to entertain the king (4)

Puzzle 12
Chifonie

Across

1 Bird shows passion in display (8)
5 Fuss about a soldier's movement (6)
9 Inscription put German leader in happier disposition (8)
10 Be prone to interrupt umpire in break (6)
11 Box for China? (3,5)
12 Furtive miss appears in court (6)
14 'Arry takes part in a scam? That's surprising! (10)
18 Corrupt grown-up English count (10)
22 'elping recovery in London (6)
23 It's hard for Tory keeping awake (4,4)
24 Deceive parent maliciously (6)
25 Tell about pastry that's going off (8)
26 Bird said to be big or little in Canadian skies (6)
27 Produce after cooking in show (8)

Down

1 Defect in porcelain has Oriental in temper (6)
2 Prophet in jail? He's upset! (6)
3 Risk of nurse taking heroin (6)
4 Plant rallied Ada's spirit (10)
6 House a large number streaming forth (8)
7 Increases subsidy? That's denied! (8)
8 Where player's not seen having bad leg (8)
13 Undertaker caught working farm machinery (10)
15 Oil producer finds primates hidden in grass (8)
16 Period abroad is a complete break (4,4)
17 Learned about colour many years ago (5,3)
19 Look round Vatican City fast (6)
20 Popular artist upset about bruise treatment (6)
21 Man said to be dark (6)

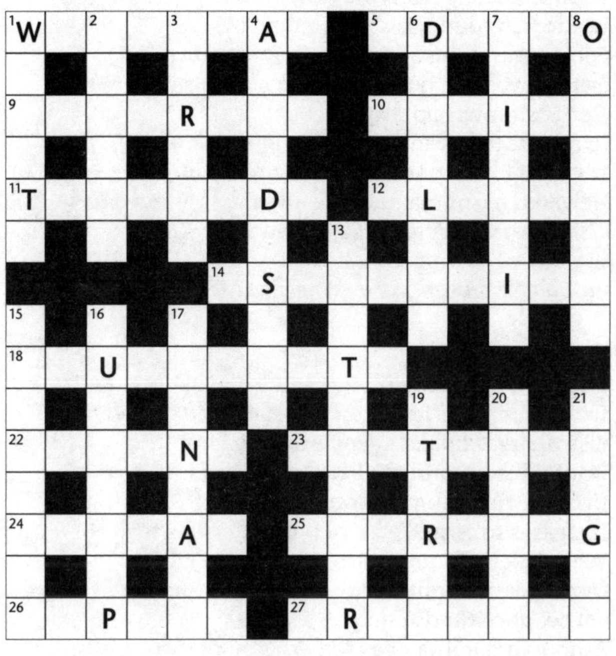

W
A
D
O
R
I
T
D
L
S
I
U
T
N
T
A
R
G
P
R

Puzzle 13
Hectence

Across

8 To get a holiday in America I hid in crumpled coat in lorry (8)
9 Consumption is covered by new support group for sickness (6)
10 Sharp butcher's knife cut out heart (6)
11 Important to see best bit (4,4)
12 Panda gestation takes a long time (4)
13 Greet second fish with rounds of applause (5,5)
15 Frets, if working gets harder (7)
16 Fruit lost colour in tart (7)
18 Dr Pasteur's solution to rodent infestation? (10)
19 In contact with posh name after returning work (4)
20 Nowadays, card game is accepted in shortened form (8)
22 Chap entered peripheries of French city (6)
23 Use an unknown convention (6)
24 Isn't a cog broken by freewheeling? (8)

Down

1 Safe from this crime during hours of darkness? (8,7)
2 First five ale vats he used for the autumn celebration (7,8)
3 Princess's bad press etc reflects insolence (10)
4 Oddly, T-shirt found in back lane entrance (7)
5 Geordie goes back to problem (4)
6 Push Ann to regret lease of property, reportedly, in a dangerous game (7,8)
7 Damn economics and cut a different position for the person next in line (6-2-7)
14 Rider's Oriental journey to find Iran, perhaps (10)
17 Fish Dad cooked in white wine (7)
21 Men taking German's unknown in America (4)

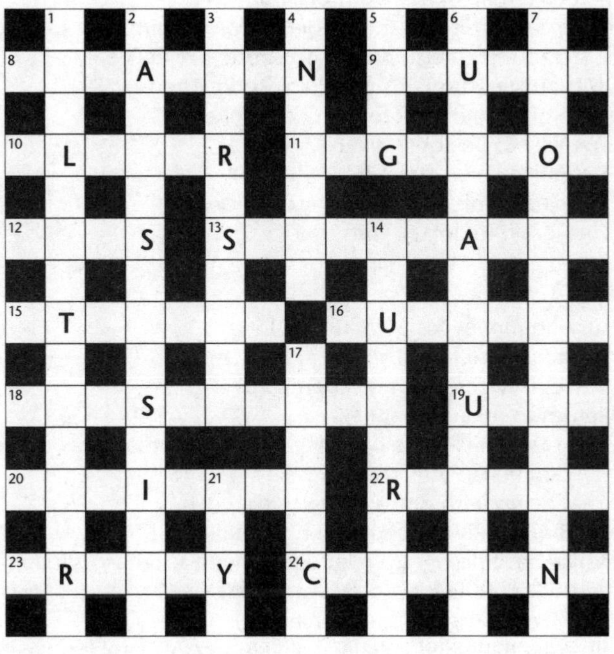

Puzzle 14

Beale

Across

9 Service woman? (9)
10 A churchman experienced pain (5)
11 Sounded agitated (7)
12 Urge one to monitor first sign of life (7)
13 Screen left in an awkward position (5)
14 Misgiving arises when one gets involved with cops in US (9)
16 It's cracking entertainment on sports day (3-3-5,4)
19 Without question, it's good advice for Thomas (9)
21 Term of endearment for favourite chap (5)
22 The way to be aggressive? (7)
23 Definitive horse race (7)
24 Woman caught with foreign currency (5)
25 Forbidden to doctor films of it (3,6)

Down

1 Lacking money for a biscuit (10)
2 Sound way to interrupt the judge's verdict (8)
3 Decided water took precedence (6)
4 Return to dreary poet (4)
5 Acts to acknowledge publicity given to charitable works (10)
6 Military action affected by foreign gain (8)
7 Cool down with one after spicy dish (6)
8 Tried generally to keep within the limit (4)
14 Nurse has to cover up relationship with another woman (10)
15 Part of pine cover used by seamstress (6,4)
17 Bird seed found by the opening (8)
18 Unusual traits one initially cultivated so as to appear creative (8)
20 Translation of Lear by one in France is not true to life (6)
21 Piano student takes drug so as to be calm (6)
22 Drift along with a newspaper (4)
23 Decanter artist removed from restaurant (4)

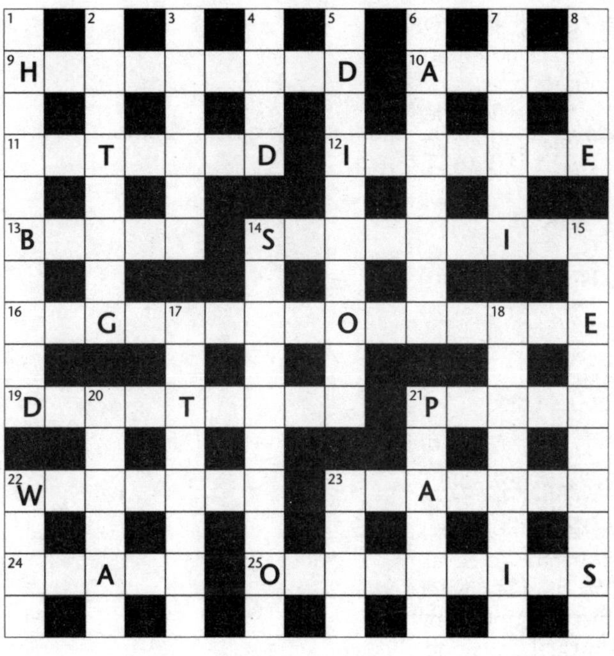

Puzzle 1
Notes and solution

Across

1 TIME(sentence)/LAG(convict)
5 LA<JO>CE (part anag)
9 FIRM(company)/GRIP(case)
10 1/MP/END
12 cryptic def
15 cryptic def
17 cryptic def
19 U(nidentified) F(lying) O(bject)
20 double def + & lit (unfair = ugly; gossip = rumour)
22 CHAP + LITERACY (anag)
26 I'M/PART
27 cryptic def
28 E/ASTER
29 KNEW CRY (anag)

Down

1 TO/FF
2 double def
3 double def
4 GO IN/G
6 IMPART (anag)
7 cryptic def
8 cryptic def
11 score = 20
13 cf case as in grammar
14 cryptic def
16 LEG/BYE
18 double def
21 double def
23 TWO IN (anag)
24 double def (cf cube root)
25 KEEL (rev)

T	I	M	E	L	A	G	■	■	C	A	J	O	L	E
O	■	A	■	I	■	O	■	■	■	R	■	P	■	L
F	I	R	M	G	R	I	P	■	I	M	P	E	N	D
F	■	K	■	H	■	N	■	T	■	P	■	N	■	E
■	■	■	S	T	A	G	E	W	H	I	S	P	E	R
A	■	H	■	S	■	■	■	E	■	T	■	R	■	B
C	H	O	R	U	S	L	I	N	E	■	■	I	C	E
C	■	R	■	P	■	E	■	T	■	H	■	S	■	R
U	F	O	■	■	U	G	L	Y	R	U	M	O	U	R
S	■	S	■	D	■	B	■	■	■	M	■	N	■	Y
A	R	C	H	E	T	Y	P	I	C	A	L	■	■	■
T	■	O	■	G	■	E	■	N	■	N	■	C	■	L
I	M	P	A	R	T	■	A	T	T	I	T	U	D	E
V	■	E	■	E	■	■	■	O	■	T	■	B	■	E
E	A	S	T	E	R	■	■	W	R	Y	N	E	C	K

Puzzle 2
Notes and solution

Across

1 POSTER ETC (anag)
6 nunS WIMper (hidden)
10 O<IT>AP (all rev) (senior citizen = OAP; that thing = it)
11 LIFT OR LIE (anag)
12 A/L/LEG/RO(se)
13 IN<HER>ES
14 AS I LOCK THE PIN (anag)
17 OVER/A BUN/DANCE
21 TOPER OH (anag)
22 AB/R/EAST
24 DOG OWNER R (anag)
25 piece/peace (homophone)
26 T/ONE
27 THE BR/O/ADS

Down

1 PA BOTTLE (anag)
2 LATE/P (all rev) (dead = late; poppy head = P)
3 cryptic def & double def
4 ROOT(source) OUT(abroad/not in)
5 T<ALL>IES
7 NEW RAFTER (anag)
8 MO/ROSE (doctor = MO)
9 PRINTER DO GRAPH (anag)
15 CL<OS/E D>OWN (big = OS; editor = ed; comic = clown)
16 HE/ATHENS
18 AIR/PORT
19 cryptic def & double def
20 S/TO W/IT (second = S; that is to say = to wit)
23 ACE RA (all rev)

Puzzle 3
Notes and solution

Across

1 PASSED (anag) (major suit at bridge)
5 cryptic def
9 FOX/GLOVE
10 CRUEL(anag) + S(uppurating)
11 ITALIAN TAROT (anag)
13 double def
14 NATION/A/L
17 FAL/SET TO
18 fEEL Slippery (hidden)
20 PRISON SEARCH (anag)
23 THE BAR (anag)
24 cryptic def
25 REP/RISES (salesman = rep; gets up = rises)
26 TALE/NT

Down

2 double def
3 DIGIT/ALI'S
4 double def
5 double def
6 SUBTLE IT (anag)
7 R<ACE>R
8 cryptic def
12 THE LEAD ETC (anag)
15 cryptic def (lighter = a spill)
16 STOP/GAPS
19 THRONE (anag)
21 cf Inter Milan
22 PLAN(e)

S	P	A	D	E	S		S	U	B	G	R	O	U	P
	L		I		M		M		L		A		N	
F	O	X	G	L	O	V	E		U	L	C	E	R	S
	T		I		O		L		E		E		E	
			T	O	T	A	L	I	T	A	R	I	A	N
	D		A		H		I		I				D	
D	E	A	L				N	A	T	I	O	N	A	L
	C		I		S		G		S		V		B	
F	A	L	S	E	T	T	O				E	E	L	S
	T				O		F		H		R		E	
C	H	A	I	R	P	E	R	S	O	N	S			
	L		N		G		O		R		P		P	
B	E	R	T	H	A		S	U	N	D	I	A	L	S
	T		E		P		E		E		L		A	
R	E	P	R	I	S	E	S		T	A	L	E	N	T

Puzzle 4
Notes and solution

Across

1 OR PASTURE (anag)
6 might/widow's mite (homophone)
9 UGLY IRAQ NO FUN I'D (anag)
10 ALLE(y) (rev)
11 THE E/MEN(rev)/Y (Time is the enemy) (you = thee; workers = men; (holida)Y)
14 A/N/DAN/TIN/O (new = n; fellow = Dan; can = tin; O(perate))
15 SPRU(c)E
16 H<ORE>B
18 CO/(a)GITATOR
20 L(i)KELY END (anag)
21 SCAR(y)
25 ILLEGAL ENTRANT I (anag)
26 GIS(rev)/MA (sigma = letter from abroad; GIs = soldiers)
27 HOUND READ (Spoonerism)

Down

1 double def
2 ENA/BLED (homophone)
3,17 OTIS (lift company) RED (= revolutionary) /DING (= sound)
4 revolutionARY Lefties (hidden)
5 cryptic def & double def
6 MARTENSITE (used in making steel)/place for martens (tree mammals) to live
7 double def (listener = ear)
8 T<EDDY/B>EAR (twist = eddy; B(reak); split = tear)
12 Latin phrase for 'not present'
13 cryptic def
14 IN HEAT<A/N>S (part anag) (a + number = n in anag)
19 T<ACT>ILE (tile = hat = Derby)
22 RAG/ED
23 bow/beau (homophone)
24 F(i)RED (ego = I)

P	T	E	R	O	S	A	U	R		M	I	G	H	T
I		N		T		R		U		A		L		E
Q	U	A	L	I	F	Y	I	N	G	R	O	U	N	D
U		B		S		L		T		T		E		D
E	L	L	A				T	H	E	E	N	E	M	Y
		E		I		F		R		N		A		B
A	N	D	A	N	T	I	N	O		S	P	R	U	E
T				A		S		U		I				A
H	O	R	E	B		C	O	G	I	T	A	T	O	R
E		E		S		A		H		E		A		
N	E	D	K	E	L	L	Y				S	C	A	R
I		D		N		Y		B		F		T		A
A	L	I	T	T	L	E	L	E	A	R	N	I	N	G
N		N		I		A		A		E		L		E
S	I	G	M	A		R	O	U	N	D	H	E	A	D

Puzzle 5
Notes and solution

Across

1 PO<TEN>T
4 double def
9 COME UP/SCOTCH TAR (part anag)
10 MAD POE (anag)
11 POI<NAG(part anag)NT
12 R<EVER>SAL (always = ever; right = r; girl = Sal)
14 SEE PAL (anag)
15 RE CART (all rev)
18 WE DO IT UP (anag)
21 PAR/LANCE
22 double def
24 CHATS/WORTH HOUSE (Charles Worth, 1825–95)
25 ST/ROLL (way = st(reet))
26 US/FUEL (part anag)

Down

1 PRO/POSE
2 nesT REMAins (hidden)
3 double def
5 A/SCRIBE
6 TRAIN/BAND (old English militia)
7 RE<CAN>ST (part anag) (is able to = can + anag)
8 COMP + EL
13 ORACLES AT (anag)
16 RE-ACHES
17 RENE/LAW(rev)
18 W<HER>RY (turned aside = wry; female = her)
19 double def
20 UT/LINES (part anag) (ut = note in music)
23 double def

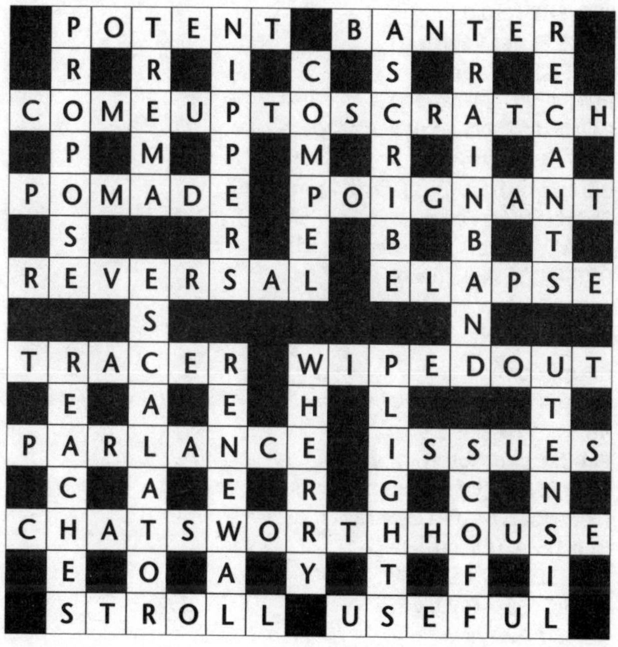
POTENT
BANTER
COMEUPTOSCRATCH
POMADE
POIGNANT
REVERSAL
ELAPSE
TRACER
WIPEDOUT
PARLANCE
ISSUES
CHATSWORTHHOUSE
STROLL
USEFUL

Puzzle 6
Notes and solution

Across

1 GENERAL (= rough) + STAFF (= man, as a verb)
8 double def
9 NATIVE M(arsh) (anag)
11 DI'S/TORT (legal wrong = tort)
12 LETTERS (anag)
13 riTA'S TEnet (hidden)
14 I BET ARNIE (anag)
16 I SANG A LOT (anag)
19 GU(ards)/LAG (convict = lag)
21 BREAD IS (anag)
23 LA/N(oisy)/G(angs)/OUR (part anag)
24 GENT/EEL
25 TREAD/LE(vers) (press = tread)
26 E(ffectiv)E NEW RANGERS (anag)

Down

1 double def
2 NOIS<OM>E (rumour = noise; title = O(rder) of M(erit))
3 RIGHT WIN/G
4 SEVILle (hidden rev)
5 THE/AT/ER (US spelling)
6 (reprobat)E + FALLEN (anag)
7 BANDS A TOGGLE (anag)
10 MARKET(sell) GARDEN(plot)
15 (brocad)E + PAULETTE
17 S/C<ANNE>/R
18 AUSTER (Paul Auster) + E
19 SING(part anag)/ENG
20 L/A/UNDER
22 D(etective)/E(xamine)/L(eads)/V(ital)/E(vidence) (initials)

		G	E	N	E	R	A	L	S	T	A	F	F	
G		R		O		I		I		H		E		
L	E	A	N	I	N	G		V	I	E	T	N	A	M
A		S		S		H		E		A		E		A
D	I	S	T	O	R	T		S	E	T	T	L	E	R
S		E		M		W				E		L		K
T	A	S	T	E		I	N	E	B	R	I	A	T	E
O						N		P						T
N	O	S	T	A	L	G	I	A		G	U	L	A	G
E		C		U				U		I		A		A
B	R	A	I	S	E	D		L	A	N	G	U	O	R
A		N		T		E		E		S		N		D
G	E	N	T	E	E	L		T	R	E	A	D	L	E
		E		R		V		T		N		E		N
	A	R	S	E	N	E	W	E	N	G	E	R		

Puzzle 7
Notes and solution

Across

1 UN<FOR/GIVE/AB>LE (French articles = un, le; supporting = for; present = give; sailor = AB)
10 cf cricket and All Fools' Day
11 TEMPE(r) (Vale of Tempe in Greece)
12 cf spike of corn
13 EYE(look)-OPENER (1st person)
14 BY THE RA (anag)
16 RA A HELP (anag)
18 A/TT/R/ACT (abstainer = TT; right = r; performance = act)
20 DELI/G/HT
21 K<IS/S/AGRA>M (1km is over half a mile)
23 cryptic def NO/NET
24 diphTHONG (a different spoken vowel sound)
25 MAG<F/IN(both rev)>IC/O (witchcraft = magic; female = f; love = O)
26 UM/BRIAN SCHOOL (school = collective noun for fish)

Down

2 GLEN(part anag)/1/GENT
3 O/F USE (oxygen = O; melt = fuse)
4 GALLE<R>Y (take = r; cookhouse = galley)
5 VERME(s)/ER (vermes = worm structures)
6 AN/TIP/A/PAL
7 LE MON(de)
8 cryptic def
9 (h)OSPITAL ROTTEN (anag)
15 T/RAF/ALGAR(ve)
17 RATING ONE (anag)
19 TRY MASH (anag) (an Anglo-Saxon gold coin)
20 DAM/AGES
22 scientiST OR Mathematician (hidden)
23 NEIGH(bours)

	U	N	F	O	R	G	I	V	E	A	B	L	E	
C		E		F		A		E		N		E		P
L	E	G	P	U	L	L	E	R		T	E	M	P	E
O		L		S		L		M		I		O		T
S	P	I	K	E		E	Y	E	O	P	E	N	E	R
E		G				R		E		A				O
B	R	E	A	T	H	Y		R	A	P	H	A	E	L
R		N		R						A		R		S
A	T	T	R	A	C	T		D	E	L	I	G	H	T
C				F		H		A				E		A
K	I	S	S	A	G	R	A	M		N	O	N	E	T
E		T		L		Y		A		E		T		I
T	H	O	N	G		M	A	G	N	I	F	I	C	O
S		R		A		S		E		G		N		N
	U	M	B	R	I	A	N	S	C	H	O	O	L	

Puzzle 8
Notes and solution

Across

5 (I)A<NORA>K(e)
6 BATH/OS
9 CAMP/US
10 RE/VEIL/(mi)LE
11 R/I'LL
12 CON/(in)FLUENCE
13 CROSS <S>WORDS
18 cryptic def of plagiarist
21 double def
22 OAR BLADE (anag)
23 C(I)OBBER
24 N TARGE(t) (anag)
25 IN/TAKE

Down

1 COME (a)PRIL (anag)
2 BARS/AC
3 cryptic def (Twelfth Night)
4 HIKERS (anag)
5 what'll/wattle (homophone)
7 S.O. + LACE
8 TREND (= style) + SETTER (1 down = compiler)
14 SARA/BAND
15 double def
16 THO(part anag) DOG(trouble)
17 accede/axe seed (homophone)
19 ROY(man rev)/KER(b) (a delivery bowled at cricket)
20 RE<CE>NT

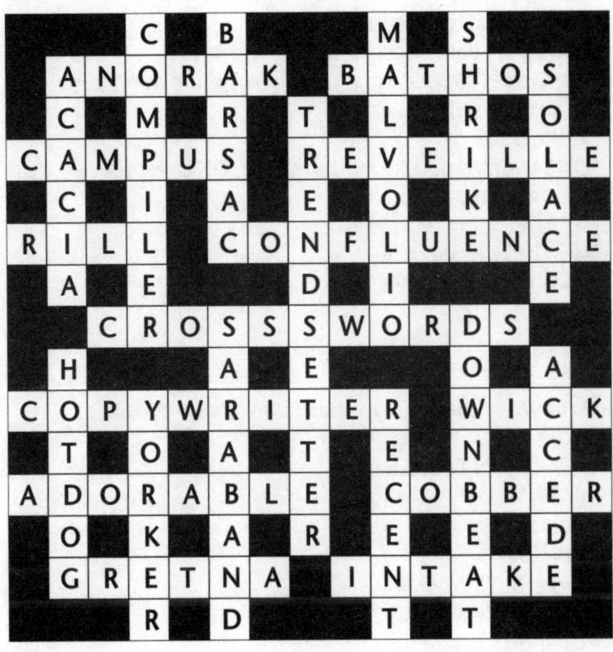

Puzzle 9
Notes and solution

Across

1 SOLE BONNE FEMME (French for good woman)
9 ANN/OUNCE/R
10 O/BRAG (all rev)
11 POOR L (anag)
12 LOVER RUDE(ly) (anag)
13 cryptic def (part of common logarithm)
14 double def (Chosen was former name for Korea)
17 UNTIDY (anag)
19 L<ACROSS>E
22 SIG<IS>MUND (Sigmund Romberg, US composer)
24 T<REV>O (all rev)
25 EN/TRY (en = half an em)
26 E(vent)/L<1/MIN>ATE
27 EDGAR(6 dn) FELT HEART (anag)

Down

1 cryptic def
2 NIL/ON/A/L (all rev) (nothing = nil; pound = L)
3 double def & cryptic def
4 YE<CROPS>N (part rev)
5 (I)EARNER
6 GRADE (anag)
7 double def
8 GOOD IN/VESTMENT
15 cryptic def (Harrow School)
16 double def
18 double def
20 SEE/PAGE
21 PURE/ED
23 S/AYER (Leo Sayer; Sir Alfred Ayer, 1910–89)

S	O	L	E	B	O	N	N	E	F	E	M	M	E	
H		A		L		E		A		D		A		G
A	N	N	O	U	N	C	E	R		G	A	R	B	O
D		O		E		R		N		A		B		O
O	R	L	O	P		O	V	E	R	R	U	L	E	D
W		I		R		P		R				E		I
M	A	N	T	I	S	S	A		C	H	O	S	E	N
I				N		Y		S		A				V
N	U	D	I	T	Y		L	A	C	R	O	S	S	E
I		I				P		N		R		E		S
S	I	G	I	S	M	U	N	D		O	V	E	R	T
T		I		A		R		W		W		P		M
E	N	T	R	Y		E	L	I	M	I	N	A	T	E
R		A		E		E		C		N		G		N
	A	L	F	R	E	D	T	H	E	G	R	E	A	T

Puzzle 10
Notes and solution

Across

9 FRI/(c)AR(e)
10 CHAP ATE IT (anag)
11 OVER<EX/RE>T (public = overt; old = ex; monarch = RE (King Edward))
12 panELLISts (hidden)
13 F/LATTE/N
17,18 THICK(dumb) LIP(insolence)
20 PLAN + K
22 cryptic def
25 SH/RIVEr/L (quietly = sh; flower = river; hands = R/L)
26 HAW(-haw)/S/E (Lord Haw-Haw, the WWII traitor; front part of ship)
27 CAR<TOUCH>E
30 MOON/SHINE
31 IT(rev)/THE

Down

1 FOR A (anag) (rhyming slang for hair)
2 LIT/IRATE (part anag)
3,15 FREEMA<SON>RY
4 MATE/RN/AL (RN = service; AL = man)
5 BAN(= stop) + TAM(=woollen hat)
6 CHIEF(first) S/(fo)U(r)/PER(by)
7 STOLE/N(ovember)
8 double def
13 CH<T>EF (part anag) (time = t in anag)
14 TEA IT'S A KEY (anag)
16 YOKE/L
19 PAST/RI(t)ES (finished = PAST; acts = rites)
21 cryptic def (cf the law)
23 PO/WW<O>W (River Po, www = the net)
24 RE/COIL (about = re; ring = coil)
26 double def
28 O/AT/H
29 EVEN(t)

A		L		F		M		B		C		S		A
F	R	I	A	R		A	P	A	T	H	E	T	I	C
R		T		E		T		N		I		O		T
O	V	E	R	E	X	E	R	T		E	L	L	I	S
		R				R		A		F		E		
F	L	A	T	T	E	N		M	A	S	O	N	R	Y
E		T		A		A				U				O
T	H	I	C	K		L	I	P		P	L	A	N	K
C				E				A		E		D		E
H	A	P	P	I	E	R		S	H	R	I	V	E	L
		O		T		E		T				O		
H	A	W	S	E		C	A	R	T	O	U	C	H	E
U		W		A		O		I		A		A		V
M	O	O	N	S	H	I	N	E		T	I	T	H	E
P		W		Y		L		S		H		E		N

Puzzle 11
Notes and solution

Across

1 PASH/A
4 MO/COB(rev)/RAT (Mo Mowlam + horse = cob; turncoat = rat)
8 PO<HOT>SY/N/THESIS (flowers = posy; warm = hot; new = n; doctoral research = thesis)
10 C<HEN/ILL>E (layer = hen; in poor health = ill; church = CE)
11 COMING (anag)
12 T<PEA K(part anag)/OWER (keep = tower (as in castle); peak (anag))
15 B<ASS>O
17 PA<N/S>Y (remuneration = pay; poles = N,S)
18 ETA/I/LATER (all rev)
19 T<RAG>IC
21 TEA C<LOT>H (item for sale = lot; train = teach)
24 AUTHOR IN H(amburg) HOTEL (anag)
25 FACT/O/TUM
26 SO<L>AR (take to sky = soar; line = l)

Down

1 OP(rev)/OP(rev)/CAT/E<PET>L (works = op,op; animals = cat, pet (tame); the spanish = el)
2 SOOT/ER/KIN (imaginary afterbirth of Dutch women who huddled by stoves)
3 AL(IO>I (Io, the lover of Zeus)
4 MAY/FLOWER
5 rugBY TEam (hidden)
6 CHER<NOB>YL
7 A<X/10>M (10 = X +10; morning = AM)
9 SC/H(ungary)/OPEN<(matcH/AU>ER (to wit = sc ; player = opener; gold = AU)
13 PITY HIS SC (anag)
14 ROT/HER/HAM!
16 OVAL'S(rev)/PHIL
20 A/AMOR(part rev) (Eros = amor)
22 CAN<I>S
23 W<R>IT (jester = wit; king = R)

P	A	S	H	A	■	M	O	B	O	C	R	A	T	■
O	■	O	■	I	■	A	■	Y	■	H	■	X	■	■
P	H	O	T	O	S	Y	N	T	H	E	S	I	S	■
O	■	T	■	L	■	F	■	E	■	R	■	O	■	S
C	H	E	N	I	L	L	E	■	G	N	O	M	I	C
A	■	R	■	■	■	O	■	■	■	O	■	■	■	H
T	A	K	E	P	O	W	E	R	■	B	A	S	S	O
E	■	I	■	H	■	E	■	O	■	Y	■	L	■	P
P	A	N	S	Y	■	R	E	T	A	L	I	A	T	E
E	■	■	■	C	■	■	■	H	■	■	■	V	■	N
T	R	A	G	I	C	■	T	E	A	C	L	O	T	H
L	■	R	■	S	■	W	■	R	■	A	■	P	■	A
■	H	O	L	I	E	R	T	H	A	N	T	H	O	U
■	■	M	■	S	■	I	■	A	■	I	■	I	■	E
■	F	A	C	T	O	T	U	M	■	S	O	L	A	R

Puzzle 12
Notes and solution

Across

1 W<HEAT>EAR (passion = heat; display = wear)
5 AD<A/GI>O (fuss = ado; soldier = GI)
9 G HAPPIER (anag)
10 RE<LIE>F (be prone = lie; umpire = ref)
11 cryptic def (China tea)
12 C<LOSE>T (miss = lose; court = ct)
14 A/ST<(h)OUND>ING (h(arry) = h(ound); scam = sting)
18 ADULT/E/RATE
22 (h)EALING
23 C<AST IR>ON (Tory = Con; awake = astir)
24 PARENT (anag)
25 S<TART>ING (tell = sing; pastry = tart)
26 double def (Big/Little Dipper = Ursa Major/Minor in NA)
27 A<AFTER(part anag)/CT (after (anag) in show = act)

Down

1 WR<E>ATH
2 JAIL + HE (anag)
3 T<H>REAT (nurse = treat; heroin = H)
4 ADA'S SPIRIT (anag)
6 D/WELLING
7 GAINS/AID
8 OFF(bad)/STAGE(leg)
13 C/ON/TRACTOR (caught = c; working = on)
15 R<APES>EED
16 double def (period = a full stop in American English)
17 S<TONE> AGE
19 STAR<V>E
20 IN/RA(both rev)/CA
21 knight/night (homophone)

W	H	E	A	T	E	A	R		A	D	A	G	I	O
R		L		H		S				W		A		F
E	P	I	G	R	A	P	H		R	E	L	I	E	F
A		J		E		I				L		N		S
T	E	A	C	A	D	D	Y		C	L	O	S	E	T
H		H		T		I		C		I		A		A
					A	S	T	O	U	N	D	I	N	G
R		F		S		T		N		G		D		E
A	D	U	L	T	E	R	A	T	E					
P		L		O		A		R		S		A		K
E	A	L	I	N	G		C	A	S	T	I	R	O	N
S		S		E				C		A		N		I
E	N	T	R	A	P		S	T	A	R	T	I	N	G
E		O		G				O		V		C		H
D	I	P	P	E	R		A	R	T	E	F	A	C	T

Puzzle 13
Notes and solution

Across

8 VA<COA<<I>>T(part anag)>N
9 N/A<USE>A (AA = Alcoholics Anonymous)
10 CLE(a)VER
11 HIGH(important) SPOT(see)
12 pandA GEStation (hidden)
13 S/HAKE/ HANDS
15 FRETS IF (anag)
16 CUR<RAN>T
18 MO/PASTEUR (part anag)
19 U/OP(part rev)/N (posh = U; name = n; work = op)
20 A<BRIDGE>D
22 R<HE>IMS
23 TREAT/Y
24 ISN'T A COG (anag)

Down

1 cryptic def
2 FIRST V ALE VATS HE (anag)
3 DI PRESS ETC (anag)
4 LA<T(s)H(i)R(t)>NE (part anag)
5 GANS (rev) (NE dialect for goes)
6 rush Ann rue let (all homophones)
7 DAMN ECONOMICS (a)ND (anag)
14 E/QUEST/IRAN (part anag)
17 H<DAD(part anag)>OCK
21 G/U<Y>S (German = G; unknown = y; American = US)

	D		H		D		E		S		R		S	
V	A	C	A	T	I	O	N		N	A	U	S	E	A
	Y		R		S		T		A		S		C	
C	L	E	V	E	R		H	I	G	H	S	P	O	T
	I		E		E		R				I		N	
A	G	E	S		S	H	A	K	E	H	A	N	D	S
	H		T		P		L		Q		N		I	
S	T	I	F	F	E	R		C	U	R	R	A	N	T
	R		E		C		H		E		O		C	
M	O	U	S	E	T	R	A	P	S		U	P	O	N
	B		T				D		T		L		M	
A	B	R	I	D	G	E	D		R	H	E	I	M	S
	E		V		U		O		I		T		A	
T	R	E	A	T	Y		C	O	A	S	T	I	N	G
	Y		L		S		K		N		E		D	

Puzzle 14
Notes and solution

Across

9 cryptic def
10 A/CH/ED
11 double def
12 1/M(onitor)PULSE
13 B<L>IND
14 1 COPS IN US (anag)
16 cryptic def
19 double def & cryptic def (doubting Thomas)
21 PET/AL
22 cryptic def
23 double def
24 FRAN/C
25 FILMS OF IT (anag)

Down

1 SHORT/BREAD
2 RU<ST>LING
3 SEA/LED
4 DRAB (rev)
5 AD/MISSIONS
6 CAMP/GAIN (part anag)
7 CHILL/1
8 triED GEnerally (hidden)
14 SISTER/HOOD
15 NEEDLE(pine part) CASE(cover)
17 NUT/HATCH
18 TRAITS 1 C(ultivated) (anag)
20 UN + LEAR (part anag)
21 P/L/ACID
22 W/A/FT (with = w; newspaper = FT (Financial Times))
23 CA(ra)FE

S		R		S		B		A		C		C		E
H	O	U	S	E	M	A	I	D		A	C	H	E	D
O		S		A		R		M		M		I		G
R	A	T	T	L	E	D		I	M	P	U	L	S	E
T		L		E				S		A		L		
B	L	I	N	D		S	U	S	P	I	C	I	O	N
R		N				I		I		G				E
E	G	G	A	N	D	S	P	O	O	N	R	A	C	E
A				U		T		N				R		D
D	O	U	B	T	L	E	S	S		P	E	T	A	L
		N		H		R				L		I		E
W	A	R	P	A	T	H		C	L	A	S	S	I	C
A		E		T		O		A		C		T		A
F	R	A	N	C		O	F	F	L	I	M	I	T	S
T		L		H		D		E		D		C		E

List of common abbreviations

A	above, acre, answer, alto, Austria, (kind of) bomb
AA	drivers, non-drinkers
AB	sailor, salt, tar
AC	account, current
AD	bill, notice, modern, nowadays
AG	silver
AI	first class, main road
AL	aluminium, Capone, Jolson
AM	American, morning
AS	Anglo-Saxon, arsenic
AU	gold
AV	authorised version, Bible
B	bishop, book, born, bowled, British, second-class
BA	fliers, graduate, scholar
BB	Brigitte Bardot, very soft
BBC	TV, radio, auntie
BC	old times
BM	(British) museum

BMA	doctors
BO	personal problem
BR	Britain, brother
BT	baronet
C	about, carbon, caught, Celsius, century, chapter, club, cold, Conservative, 100
CA	about, accountant, calcium, California
CAPT	captain, officer
CB	companion (of the Bath)
CBE	companion (of the British Empire)
CC	quantity, volume, 200
CD	diplomats
CE	church (of England), establishment
CF	carry forward, compare with
CH	child, church, companion (of Honour), Switzerland
CHEM	chemical, chemistry
CI	Channel Islands
CIA	spies
CL	chlorine, 150
CO	care of, cobalt, (commanding) officer, Colorado, company, firm
COD	cash on delivery
COL	colonel, officer
COY	company
CPL	corporal
CR	chromium, credit
CS	caesium, civil service
CT	caught, court
CWT	(hundred)weight
CU	copper
D	day, daughter, died/dead, diamond, (old) coin/copper, 500

DA	lawyer (American)
DB	noise (decibel)
DC	current, district commissioner, District of Columbia
DD	clergyman
DEC	deceased, December, declared
DEM	Democrat
DI	detective, policeman
DIY	home help
DNA	genes
DO	ditto
DR	medic
E	earth, east, energy, English, orient(al), point, quarter
EA	each, East Africa/Anglia
EC	city (of London)
ED	editor, newsman
EG	for example, say
ENG	engineer, England/English
ENT	hospital department
EP	epistle, letter, record
ER	(with) hesitation
ET	extra-terrestrial, alien
ETA	terrorists (Basque)
EX	earlier, former lover/spouse
F	Fahrenheit, fellow, female, fine, fluorine, folio, Friday, loud
FA	footballers, Fanny Adams (nothing)
FE	iron
FF	folios, pages, very loud
FO	Foreign Office, diplomats
FR	father, French
FT	foot/feet

G	good, gramme, lightweight, gravity, force
GA	Georgia, state
GB	Britain
GG	(child's) horse
GI	soldier (US)
GK	Greek
GP	doctor, group
GR	grain, grand, great, Greece
H	hard, height, Henry, hospital, hot, hotel, hour, hydrogen, (kind of) bomb
HA	hectare, area
HAL	prince
HB	pencil
HE	ambassador, governor, (high) explosive, helium
HG	mercury
HM	the Queen, harbour master
HO	house, Home Office
HP	(horse) power, never-never, sauce, Parliament,
HQ	headquarters
HR	hour
HT	high tension
I	first person, iodine, one, single, unit
IC	in charge, 99
ID	I would
IE	that is, that's
II	eleven, side, team
ILL	I will
IM	I am
IO	ten
IQ	intelligence
IRA	terrorists (Irish)

IS	island
IT	Italian
IV	4
IX	9
J	jack, Japan, joule, judge
JM	Barrie
JO	little woman
JOR	Jordan
JP	magistrate
K	constant, kelvin, killed, kilo, king, potassium, rex, 1,000
KC	kilocycle, old lawyer
KG	knight (of the Garter)
KO	kick off, knock out
KT	knight, knot
KY	Kentucky, state
L	lake, large, Latin, learner, beginner, pupil, left, liberal, little, long, love, pound, sovereign, 50
LA	Los Angeles
LAB	Labour
LAT	Latin, latitude
LB	pound
LIB	Liberal
LP	record
LSD	drug, (old) money
LT	lieutenant, officer
M	maiden, male, married, metre, motorway, Frenchman, 1,000
MA	degree, graduate, scholar, mother
MB	medic
MBE	decoration

MC	master of ceremonies
MD	medic
MED	medical, medicine, medium, Mediterranean, sea
MI	main road, motorway
MM	decoration, millimetre, Frenchmen
MO	medic, short time
MP	politician, military policeman, redcap
MS	manuscript, papers, writing
N	knight, name, nitrogen, noon, north, noun, point, pole, bearing, direction
NA	sodium
NB	note
NE	neon, Tyneside
NG	no/not good
NI	nickel, Ulster
NL	the Netherlands
NT	books (of the Bible)
NY	New York, state
NZ	New Zealand
O	oxygen, ball, circle, duck, love, nothing, ring, round, sphere
OB	old boy, alumnus, obiit, died
OC	officer commanding
OG	old German, own goal
OM	decoration, Order of Merit
OO	spectacles
OP	(small) operation, work
OR	gold, yellow
OT	books (of the Bible)
OS	outsize, large, sailor
OZ	Australia, ounce

P	page, parking, phosphorus, penny, small change, piano, soft(ly), president, prince
PA	father, Press Association, journalists
PB	lead
PC	copper, policeman, politically correct, Privy Council(lor)
PE	exercise, training
PH	acidity
PL	plural
PO	post office
PP	pages, very softly
PR	price, public relations
PRO	spin doctor
PS	afterthought, second thoughts
PT	exercise, training
Q	queen, question
QC	lawyer, silk
R	king, queen, monarch, regina, rex, right, river, royal, run(s), take
RA	artist(s), radium, Royal Artillery, gunners
RAC	drivers
RC	church, Red Cross
RD	road
RE	(Royal) Engineers, sappers
REP	Republican, (travelling) salesman
REV	priest, vicar
RI	religious instruction, Rhode Island, state
RM	(Royal) Marine(s), jolly
RN	(Royal) Navy, sailors
RR	(posh) car, right reverend, bishop
RT	radio telephone, right
RU	rugby (union)

RV	(revised version of) the Bible, meeting place, tryst
RY	(railway) lines
S	saint, second(s), south, pole, point, bearing, direction, shilling, old money, bob, society, small, sulphur, son, sun
SA	South Africa, sex appeal
SC	Scotland, scandium
SCH	school
SE	Home Counties, Kent
SN	tin
SO	south, standing order
SP	starting price, (betting) odds
SS	saints, ship, Sunday school, Nazis
ST	saint, good man, street, way
SW	Devon and Cornwall
T	time, kind of junction/model/shirt/square, ton
TA	army, reservists, terriers, thanks
TE	Lawrence
TH	Thursday
TT	abstainer, (Isle of Man) race
TI	titanium
TU	Tuesday
TUC	unions, workers
U	universal, university, uranium, socially acceptable, posh, kind of bend/turn
UHT	milk
ULT	ultimate(ly), ultimo, last month
UN	international organisation, peacekeepers, world council
US	America, unserviceable
USS	(American) ship

V	against, see, sign, Vatican City, verse, versus, very, victory, volts, volume, 5
VA	Virginia, state
VAT	tax
VC	decoration
VE	day of victory
VI	(flying) bomb, 6
VIP	very important person, star
VJ	day of victory
VOL	volume
VP	vice president
W	watts, west(ern), point, direction, bearing, occident(al), tungsten, Wales/Welsh, white, wicket, wide, wife, with
WC	West End, lavatory, john
WED	Wednesday
WG	Grace
WI	Mayfair, West Indies, women's institute, organised women
X	cross, kiss, multiply by, vote, unknown, wrong, 10
XI	eleven, side, team
XL	(extra) large, 40
XV	fifteen, side, team
XX	score, 20
Y	yard, year, yen, penultimate, unknown
YR	year, your
Z	last, omega, zero
ZA	South Africa
ZN	zinc
ZZ	asleep, snoring

Other reading

Barnard, D.St.P., *Anatomy of the Crossword* (Bell, 1963)

Campbell, J.M. (ed), *Torquemada: 112 Best Crossword Puzzles* (Pushkin Press, 1942)

Clère, J.J., 'Acrostiches et Mots Croisés des Anciens Egyptiens' in *Chronique d'Égypte*, 25 January 1938

Crisp, Ruth, *Crosswords: How to Solve Them* (Hodder & Stoughton, 1992)

Macnutt, D.S. (with Alec Robins), *Ximenes on the Art of the Crossword* (Methuen, 1966; republished 2001)

Manley, Don, *Chambers Crossword Manual* (Chambers, 1986; new editions 1992 and 2001)

Millington, Roger, *The Strange World of the Crossword* (M & J Hobbs in association with Michael Joseph, 1974; republished 1976)

Putnam, Don, *Crossword Solving* (EP Publishing, 1975)

Robins, Alec, *Teach Yourself Crosswords* (Hodder & Stoughton, 1975; republished as *The ABC of Crosswords*, Corgi, 1981)

The Penguin Book of The Times 50th Anniversary Crosswords (1980)

Torquemada, *The Torquemada Puzzle Book: A Miscellany* (Victor Gollancz, 1934)

Zandee, J., *An Ancient Egyptian Crossword Puzzle* (Ex Oriente Lux, 1966)